# One Million Minutes

## What My Daughter Taught Me About Time

# WOLF KUPER

Translation by Imogen Taylor

Published by Lagom
An imprint of Bonnier Books UK
3.08, The Plaza,
535 Kings Road,
Chelsea Harbour,
London, SW10 0SZ

www.bonnierbooks.co.uk

Hardback ISBN 978-1-78870-105-1
eBook ISBN 978-1-78870-106-8

A CIP catalogue of this book is available from the British Library.
Doodles by Dominic Robson (page 29, 36, 39, 41, 172)
Designed by Envy Design
Illustrations by Martina Frank
Translation by Imogen Taylor

Printed and bound in Great Britain by Clays Ltd, Elcograf S.p.A.

1 3 5 7 9 10 8 6 4 2

Thank you to Nina for believing that dreams are possible; to Vera and Simon for helping me to smile about the things that may not change; and to our wonderful life for teaching me how to tell one from the other.

# CONTENTS

Prologue                                          ix

The Chance of My Life                             1

What's Wet and Falls from the Sky?               14

No Stresstic                                      22

Time Travellers                                   31

Downsizing                                        37

In Search of the Really Nice Things              48

Same Same but Different                           59

Stone Lettuce                                     71

Shortcut to Someday                               78

Fisherman, Fisherman, How Deep is the Water?     89

Michael and the Lightness of Being              100

Peace and Freedom and All That                  111

Mud. Brick. Home                                123

Child's Play                                     135

Real Men                                         143

You Never Run Alone                              153

The Watershed                     164
Home Sweet Home                   173
Lake Tekapo                       182
La Vida es un Carnaval            194
Epilogue                          204
Afterword                         209
Acknowledgements                  213

# PROLOGUE

IT WOULDN'T BE QUITE FAIR TO BLAME DR K. F. Finkelbach for my present situation. I am lying in a hammock on a beach, on a remote island south of the border between Thailand and Myanmar; I have, in fact, been lying here every day for the last 72,331 minutes, the children beside me, playing quietly (for the moment, at least), and beside them, four big bags of shells and other remnants of strange and exotic sea creatures. Apart from anything else, blame is the wrong word, given the gratifying nature of the situation – certainly compared with the kind of stuff I'd be doing if my life had continued along normal lines and I were still travelling between airport lounges, hotels and conference centres. But things have turned out differently for all of us: no school, no work, just a life of adventure – and that does, somehow, have something to do with Dr Finkelbach.

# THE CHANCE
# OF MY LIFE

'WE HAVE TO CHANGE SOMETHING,' SAID VERA.

'Yes.'

'But when?'

I glanced at my cup of tea, dog-tired. My wife was not going to let the subject drop, even if we were relaxing on the sofa. Only that morning I'd got back from a meeting at the UN Environment Programme headquarters in Nairobi, and a few hours later I'd heard the news at the institute: the German Research Ministry's project team had decided to send me to the UN Conference of the Parties in Brazil. It was a career breakthrough for me. The most important figures in international environmental policy would be there, including several ministers and heads of state. This wasn't the kind of opportunity you turned down. Not only would I be able to present our research in person, I'd also be able to conduct unofficial informal talks that might lead to any number of exciting possibilities.

But success comes at a cost. I worked at fever pitch. Ridiculous numbers of meetings, long hours, weekend work. It felt like a kind of tunnel. One morning, waking up in a hotel, it had taken me a full ten seconds to work out where I was. More than once, I'd tried to get into our flat with my work keys.

'Now's not the time to talk about fundamental changes,' I said. 'Not so soon before the conference.'

'That's what you said before the meeting in Nairobi.'

Vera was right. This was an ongoing chain reaction. If I was working on important issues now, I was likely to be working on even more important issues in the future. Success seemed to create an endless spiral. I was juggling God knows how many projects at once. After my PhD, I had taken over running a research group in Bonn. I also had my assignments from the UN, and on top of that, I organised a collaborative research network with five foreign partners. We were among the top three global teams producing large-scale biodiversity maps; in some areas, we and our partners at the University of York were the top team. In five years of frantic work, we had mapped the biodiversity of the whole of Africa. It's a tough business; you have to be permanently on the alert to prevent your competitors from publishing before you. In fact, you have to be quicker than everyone else at just about everything. It's all about time. The only real option is to get straight into the fast lane and stay there – non-stop full throttle on the road to success. Science is one big fast race; you can almost get high on it. I was close to becoming addicted.

Vera's voice tore me out of my thoughts again.

'I'm here, Nina's here, and you – where are you? Quito, Cape Town, Nairobi – and now Brazil…'

'It's the chance of my life,' I said, a little testily.

'What do you mean by that?'

'These conferences are extremely important. Networking and all that. Everyone who's anyone will be there. UNEP, WCMC, FAO, Smithsonian, ICSU, all the…'

'No, I meant *your life*,' Vera said. 'What is this life you're talking about?'

It was no use dodging the question. I met her gaze with a patient smile.

'OK, plan A goes like this: if I accept a postdoctoral position like the one that might come up in Cape Town, we could move within six months. Once I've found my feet, we could stay maybe a year and a half, two years. By then I should have enough publications to apply for a professorship. Then I could propose projects of my own: lecture tours abroad, research projects, eventually a sabbatical – all that stuff. I can keep the UN stuff going alongside it. And you know how well it pays – we'll be rolling in it. We'll be able to afford everything. A nice apartment, eating out, expensive holidays – the works!'

And because Vera still wasn't looking at me the way I wanted her to, I added, 'It'll be a good life, won't it? It's just going to take a bit of time to make it happen.'

She looked at me sternly. 'Wolf, we already have a life. You just have to give it a chance.'

I looked at her, nonplussed. 'How do you mean?'

But she'd stood up; our talk was over.

'Don't go,' I said, reaching for her.

'Nina's woken up,' she said, stepping into the next room, where our daughter had been sleeping.

I decided I'd better leave it for now; I had another few documents to read through. After all, the next day was going to be pretty stressful.

\* \* \*

I expect that every environmental scientist dreams of getting a presentation slot at a global climate and environment summit at least once in his or her life. At the UN Conference of the Parties in the southern Brazilian city of Curitiba, thousands of delegates from all over the world were gathering for a huge crisis meeting. The agenda included environmental protection, genetic resources, climate change, land use, development work – pretty much everything.

Together with a handful of other scientists from Germany, Benin and the Ivory Coast, I'd been asked to provide information on a research programme organised by the German Ministry of Research. (A cardinal rule, when dealing with scientists and *policians* – what Nina used to call politicians – is *do not give advice*. Providing information is just about acceptable.)

It had taken me some time to get used to the rules of the political world. Recently, for example, I'd had to spend days evaluating and processing data for an FAO (the UN's Food and Agriculture Organisation) report, knowing quite well that the data in question was false. Some central African states make a habit of declaring vast tracts of non-existent forest to the FAO – forest that doesn't show up on the daily-updated high-res satellite images. These virtual forests are a good example of what are known in the business as *institutional facts*. But because these non-facts are *official*, you are duty-bound to treat them as facts. Getting to grips with such subtleties is the key to success. Someone in Nairobi had explained to me that diplomacy was based on the art of pretending not to pretend. 'Like prostitution,' he added with a smile. Equally crucial is that you maintain a professional distance, at all times. You mustn't let anything get to you. Perhaps that's another price you pay for success.

My efforts were already bearing fruit. Since doing occasional work as a UN consultant, I was, for the first time in my life, earning a lot of money. An awful lot. My weekly expenses alone were as much as the net monthly wage of a postdoctoral researcher with 12 years' academic training. Tax free. At the UN we were – no kidding – handed thick brown envelopes containing $50 bills paperclipped together in bundles of 20. It was like something in a Mafia film; the bundles didn't even fit in my wallet. These preposterous expenses allowed you to enjoy a high standard of living, with VIP lounges, first-class flights and Miles & More. And because I hardly knew what to do with all the money, I shopped my way through the duty-free aisles, never going home without an expensive present for Vera. I discovered how it feels to wear bespoke suits and welted shoes; I alternated between several watches. My favourite was a beautiful limited-edition Piaget. Whenever I needed to know the time – and when didn't I? – it gave me a small thrill to look at that watch. Sometimes on the way home I'd make a little detour to saunter past the huge glass fronts of the car salesrooms. One day, I'd surprise

Vera by going to pick her up in a sports car, preferably a shiny, dark red one...

* * *

When I arrived in Curitiba, it seemed as though the city was in a state of emergency; you'd have thought Catherine the Great was about to descend. Entire streets had been repainted, hotels were overbooked, about a third of all car owners had mutated into taxi drivers and armies of shoeshine boys had sprung up overnight with newly carpentered boxes. Sex workers had smartened themselves up, there were twice the usual number of waiters in the restaurants and the whole place was teeming with security forces, who were either zealously attending to what they thought of as public order duties, or else crowding around heads of state and high-ranking ministers. Then there was the so called 'parallel culture' – a gathering of the indigenous peoples of South America, including Amazonian tribe members. There was plenty to look at: noses pierced with arrows, lips adorned with discs the size of saucers, earlobes stretched with wooden plugs, penises in quiver-like leather holders and dangling waist-length breasts. Some of the tribes I recognised from my days as a research scientist in the tropics – the Yequana, for instance, who had sometimes turned up at our research centre, the Centro Humboldt in La Esmeralda in southern Venezuela, to laugh at us or to exchange fruit and tapir steaks for batteries and torches. These indigenous people gathered here in Curitiba had come to claim financial compensation for their resources.

In addition to this illustrious gathering, tens of thousands of environmental activists and NGO delegates had put up their stands in and around the conference centre. People were campaigning, holding protest vigils, performing small plays – it looked like some kind of enormous fair. I'd only had a quick look; I hardly had any time, and besides, it was best not to get distracted. But it was fascinating. I saw a man and two children dressed in jester costumes and gaudy patchwork hats, dripping with silver jewellery inlaid with turquoise. The jewellery was also for sale, while more chains and leather bracelets were laid out on blankets. The three of them were juggling balls between them; the father was a brilliant juggler. Where do people find the time to practise? I wondered, as I made my way to the centre in my tailored suit.

'You want try?' a voice asked. I looked around. The man was holding out a ball to me. His son looked at me expectantly.

'Take one. Your turn!'

I refused politely and walked on. I really had to be going.

Vera had rung a few moments before; unsurprisingly, it was about Nina. Immediately, I'd felt the usual knot in the stomach. Our daughter Nina is physically disabled, but so far, contrary to all medical forecasts, we had been 'lucky', as I called it. Although Nina had quite a few exotic diagnoses, she was fine; quite a happy kid, in fact. We had managed to preserve some normality in our lives. However, I had to admit that I was constantly on the road, often abroad, and when I *was* in Bonn, I spent more time at the university than at home. Over the last few months, I sensed that the situation had changed. Nina was almost five now, and it didn't look like her difficulties were going to settle down by themselves, as I had secretly hoped. Vera and I had already had several big arguments, and she had even asked me if I was away so much because I felt overwhelmed at home. Of course, I had vehemently rejected that suggestion. International environmental protection was an important issue... And every Monday morning, when I went back to work, I told myself that everything would be fine.

One day, out of the blue, Vera had handed me the car keys and asked me to take Nina to her doctor's appointment, as she couldn't make it. Nina's performance that day, during our meeting with her psychologist Dr Finkelbach, was both fabulous and surreal, and for the first time I seriously questioned whether my carefully laid plans for the future would ever work out. But even then, I had managed to downplay my concerns; perhaps my fears were simply related to the stresses of my job. Everything was just a bit too much at that point.

'The EEG results have come in. Nina doesn't have epilepsy,' said Vera.

I breathed a sigh of relief.

'But we need to talk about her psychological test results. You know, the ones from when you took her to see Dr Finkelbach?'

I checked my Piaget, and resisted the urge to ask for more information. 'I'll be back soon and then we can talk,' I said.

There was a brief pause. I could just hear our baby Simon trying to get Vera's attention in the background.

'Vera?' I said, staving off my guilt.

'I'm still here,' she said.

'I'll bring you back something nice, OK?'

Another pause.

'Good luck with your presentation,' she said.

'Yes, think of me.'

'Take care.'

I blew a kiss down the phone.

I had just three days to prepare for this big presentation. The plan for day one was to smuggle myself into one of the political negotiation conferences. Scientists, of course, have no access to these, where realpolitik takes place behind the scenes. But the night before, I had begged an entry pass from a delegate friend. Although there was no photo on it, I hoped the stewards wouldn't examine us delegates too closely once we were inside the convention centre.

My friend had given me a funny look. 'Are you sure you want to go in there?'

I thought at first he was alluding to the risk of being caught.

'It's what we spend all day every day working for, isn't it?' I said jokingly.

But he shook his head. 'The conference might not be quite what you imagine, Wolf.'

I thought I knew what he was getting at, but I was a pro. 'I won't let a bunch of smooth-talking politicians get to me,' I said with a grin.

The negotiation hall in the convention centre in Curitiba was shaped like an enormous cinema and was large enough to hold an entire Roman amphitheatre. The light was subdued and I couldn't work out where it was coming from; I could only just see the people on the other side of the hall. A sea of chairs swept away before me – endless rows of seats, curving and blurring. The master builders of all those Gothic cathedrals must have been aiming for a similar effect. Each blue chair was positioned with military precision exactly 12cm from the next – no outliers, no irregularities. (It was the absolute opposite of the show happening outside, organised by activists.) In front of every seat was a table with a small panel for microphone and headphone connections, along with various red, green and amber switches, their white lettering worn with use; only a few disconnected syllables remained, just about legible. Heavy fabrics and thick-pile carpet dampened the sound. It was as though we were completely sealed off from the outside world. As the second massive door closed behind me, I felt as if I were plunging under water; the room was so large it made a noise of its own. Or was it that the absence of noise confused my ears, filling them with a deep ambient buzz? The effect was awe-inspiring. Rather than walking normally, people seemed to glide over the carpet.

A microphone squawked: '…continue with the language for Paragraph 3.2.4.' The voice was coming from the front, where the chair of the conference and other VIPs sat on a kind of rostrum. Technicians and service personnel swarmed around us like ants. Microphones were jerked back and forth, and the clerks in the middle did their best to melt into the background. So this was the global nerve centre. Each of the people sitting here belonged to the international leadership squad who worked the big levers: we used to jokingly refer to them as 'the untouchables'. I recognised one of the top secretaries of the Convention on Biological Diversity. The day before, at the Research Ministry stand, I'd spoken to him briefly about our environmental research programmes in sub-Saharan Africa, but had the feeling that his mind was on other things. There could be no doubt, though, about the professional nature of our talk. I did a good job of pretending that this diplomatic man wasn't just pretending to listen to me, and on this dodgy basis, we had what he later called 'a very informative chat'. Within my three informative minutes, he made three brief phone calls (one of them about a hire car), gave brief instructions to his assistant, greeted someone I didn't know and removed a piece of fluff from his shiny shoe – each time beaming himself back into our conversation with some elegant but disorientated remark that made it hard to believe he'd taken a word in. Before turning to leave, he gave me a pat on the back and called me by a name that bore no resemblance to mine, but with such authority that I almost began to wonder who I was. As he moved away, I got a discreet but satisfied thumbs-up from our stand organiser, who mouthed, *Well done, Wolf.*

I also spotted deputies of the World Conservation Monitoring Centre and the UN Environment Programme. I even thought I recognised two people from the International Monetary Fund. Financiers always have a huge influence on environmental politics. There's no way round that one.

Several figures scuttled to their places and I, too, hurried to find somewhere suitable to sit. At the front, a droning voice was reading out the paragraph whose wording was to be fine-tuned.

Much rustling of photocopies. I looked at the text my delegate friend had given me.

It was then that I got quite a surprise. For a second, I even thought I'd somehow ended up with the wrong text – perhaps some NGO pamphlet I'd picked up. But the text in front of me corresponded word for word to the paragraph being read out by the droning voice. I stared at the paper. Perhaps I was expecting brilliance in such esteemed company, but what I was reading was such a pile of clichés you'd think the copy had been taken from a decades-old children's science book. I read that the rainforests were being cut down to plant soya (duh) and that as a result, the species of trees that had been growing there were dying out (you don't say). I also read that if you remove species from an ecosystem you risk destabilising the whole thing, like a tower of building blocks. This was nursery-school stuff. Surely there was no reason to spend even a second looking at a text like this, let alone discussing it with several thousand top-income delegates from across the globe?

The travesty of a discussion began at a table not far from the front – perhaps representing Equatorial Guinea. An amber light flashed, and shortly afterwards the negotiator received permission to speak. He complained that from his country's perspective, the language used in this paragraph was unbalanced. It was inappropriate to single out a particular agricultural product, he said, when many other products were cultivated on former rainforest land. The man clearly represented a country that produced a great deal of soya. The chair made a note and asked what other products he considered relevant.

The man hesitated for a second and then said, 'Livestock. Beef.'

Nine amber lamps flashed almost simultaneously. I had just witnessed the spontaneous formation of the transnational livestock lobby.

Then the negotiator of another country received permission to speak; monocultural agriculture – in the Amazon area, for example – led to, he claimed, an extremely diverse range of products, so he would suggest refraining from naming individual agricultural products altogether. Before I could even start to imagine how diverse monoculture could be, six lamps went off, with three left on.

The chair addressed the plenary: did anyone have any objections? No.

Evidently if soya didn't have to be named, beef got let off the hook too. Dog doesn't eat dog.

A comment from the front row: the term *destruction* was also inappropriate. There was no adequate scientific proof that the affected areas were irrevocably damaged. After all, there was always the option of reforestation at a later date. With oil palms, for example. It put me in mind of the famous quote that was used to describe the Congress of Vienna in 1815: *The congress dances, but does not progress.*

The next speaker shared the previous speaker's view, and added that the language needed to be completely overhauled. Her government always used the modern term *sustainable usage* rather than the outdated *deforestation*.

I gasped and braced myself for a row, but there was no objection from the floor. My consultancy meetings had prepared me for a fair amount of politicking, but this was seriously depressing.

Only ten minutes later, the internationally binding legislation originally promised had been generously replaced by the phrase *voluntary self-commitment on a national level*. Without dissent. Voluntary self-commitment was one of the few things that sometimes – despite my professionalism – kept me awake at night. The words were a blatant contradiction in terms. It's a pretty hard-nosed politician who can return from a frantic two-week meeting of several thousand delegates with nothing to offer but voluntary self-commitment (instead of firm measures or sanctions) and remain immune to public reaction. It was almost unbearable watching everything being doused in a bland sauce of political harmony and finished off with a polite garnish. Here we were, a species that believed itself to be the acme of creation, intent on celebrating its own decline. To give a rough summary of what I witnessed that day: the original paragraph was about 70 words long. Within the 95 minutes that I sat in on this spectacle, there were 22 objections and 19 amendments. It must be awfully difficult putting nothing into words.

But I'd promised not to let anything get to me, so I concentrated on pretending not to pretend – and then, suddenly, one of the NGO people burst into the hall. Somehow, in spite of the multiple security levels, he had managed to get in. The padded door crashed into the wooden panelling and he chanted loudly in broken English, shouting the same words over and over, his uncontrolled voice sounding awful in the dignified silence. He was carrying a banner, but it had got in quite a twist, and his T-shirt hung skew-whiff on his body because one of the stewards had grabbed him and was holding it tight. He tried to get to the rostrum, but the steward clung fast. So he tried to drag the steward along too, and with this weighty appendage he staggered down the central aisle, heading straight for my seat. I held my breath. Despite the low light, I could make out his contorted face. For a moment he seemed familiar to me.

He yelled, his voice cracking. 'Do you have children? Today you decide their future!'

A second steward had caught up with him and now there were two of them tugging at his arm.

'Today's your big chance, understand?' The man lost his balance and almost keeled over, but managed to right himself. He clutched the table next to me; his hands were covered in turquoise rings and leather bracelets. The juggler. I couldn't tell whether he'd recognised me; it seemed unlikely, but now he was yelling right in my face – of course he was; he thought I was a delegate. 'And *you*? Do *you* have children? *Do* you?'

But now there were three stewards, who swung him right off the ground and turned to make for the door, with him in tow. The juggler's T-shirt had slipped up to his chest, revealing a sagging belly.

One of the stewards threw me an apologetic glance. 'So sorry, sir,' he said, almost saluting me. The juggler went on shouting the same thing over and over, until his voice was swallowed by the padded doors.

Now I felt weak at the knees. But there was no reaction from the delegates. Not so much as the shake of a head. The officials up on the rostrum turned the pages of their documents. Fewer than five seconds after the doors had closed behind the struggling group, the microphone voice began to drone again. It made no comment on the interruption. 'We continue with the language for Paragraph...'

*   *   *

Vera looked tired and had a we-have-to-talk look on her face when I came home. We sat together on the sofa and drank tea. I didn't notice the envelopes on the coffee table in front of us until I saw her eyes resting on them. Presumably these were the medical reports she had mentioned on the phone. Instead of responding to the obvious,

I placed my little present on top of the envelopes and looked at her encouragingly.

After a moment's hesitation, Vera unwrapped the little packet I had bought her in Madrid airport on the outward flight, and for a while she stared at the jewellery in her hand. Then, instead of putting the pendant around her neck, she placed it carefully on the coffee table, next to the envelopes. The chain coiled in a small silver circle.

Then she made a few attempts at a well-intentioned preamble. *Your work means so much to you and you're right, it is important. It isn't as if… The thing is, for me it would be… But it's also important to… If you…* But she couldn't get out the words she really wanted to say, and started again. *I do see that you…* The teacup shook slightly in her hand. Then she abandoned the bungled efforts to speak her mind and looked away. There was nothing to see outside the window, as it was already dark by the time I'd arrived.

'Wolf, we cannot go on living like this.'

The tea was too hot to drink, but she took a sip as if to steel herself. 'We will have to change,' she said.

It wasn't even a question or a proposition. I felt overwhelmed; I was only just back, and had barely processed the conference and the long flight home from Brazil. My thoughts circled. This was just not the moment for the kind of changes Vera probably meant. A career is like a bicycle. If you stop, you tip over. You give it all or nothing. On the other hand, I sensed that we were approaching a point where my avoidance strategies were no longer working. I was successful, but we were unhappy. I tried to formulate some kind of answer, feeling helpless.

Vera reached for the larger of the two envelopes and placed it on my lap. As if she had guessed my thoughts, she added: 'Maybe this will help you to decide. I see it as a chance.'

# WHAT'S WET AND FALLS FROM THE SKY?

## DR FINKELBACH'S PRACTICE
## BONN (50°44'N, 7°5' E)
## RHINELAND, GERMANY

I STARED AT THE MANILA ENVELOPE IN MY LAP. IT looked relatively mundane, the sort that usually contains junk mail or a bill. I pulled it open and scanned the contents. As I'd expected, it was from the clinic where Dr Finkelbach practised. Nevertheless, I felt completely unprepared for this moment, even though we had been anticipating it for a long time.

Dr Finkelbach was the highly acclaimed psychologist who had carried out the first cognitive-perceptual tests with Nina. His walls were hung with an impressive number of framed certificates attesting to his specialist training in work with all kinds of children, and he was an authority on carrying out – and indeed, helping to devise – intelligence and behavioural tests. He was also, crucially, in an excellent mood on the day I had taken Nina to see him – or perhaps he had made up his mind to be (and if anyone can choose their mood, a psychologist should be able to).

To demonstrate his good humour, he had leant back in his chair after each of his questions, emphatically at ease. It seemed to me that he was trying maybe just a little too hard. Nina's first four answers had thrown him, I could tell; I had more than once caught a start, the shadow of a frown, a telltale twitch in his left eye.

But a seasoned psychologist is not so easily put off his stride, and he posed question number five with a flourish. 'So, Nina. I would like you to tell me this. What's wet and falls from the sky?'

Opposite him, rather small for the rather large office chair and sitting up very straight, was the test subject – according to her earlier medical report, *a delicate, situationally sensitive girl, initially somewhat reserved and unsure of herself in contact situations, but subsequently very lively and cooperative.* Nina was listening attentively; she wrinkled her nose a little at the question, the way she always does when she's thinking.

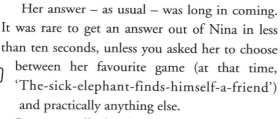

Her answer – as usual – was long in coming. It was rare to get an answer out of Nina in less than ten seconds, unless you asked her to choose between her favourite game (at that time, 'The-sick-elephant-finds-himself-a-friend') and practically anything else.

But eventually, her little nose relaxed; she was ready. Dr Finkelbach raised his eyebrows higher and higher, waiting for the right word for that wet stuff that falls from the sky. What was it?

'A dog,' the child said triumphantly, fixing her gaze on Dr Finkelbach intently, as if to be sure not to miss his reaction. I burst out laughing, earning a half-despairing, half-exasperated glance from Dr Finkelbach, and then hurriedly resumed a more serious expression. Thanks to my job, this was something I was quite good at; I had a lot of dealings with very important people, and if there's one thing you have to be with VIPs, it's serious. *Never be in a better mood than your client* is rule number one in consultancy, especially if your client is a politician.

Dr Finkelbach looked helplessly at Nina for a moment. Then he got a grip on himself and added, 'Why don't you think again, Nina? It's very wet' – he paused meaningfully – 'and it falls from the sky.' His high forehead was gleaming a little – perhaps from the rain.

But he was mistaken if he thought he could get Nina to change her mind. She cheerfully insisted on the dog, repeating her answer with the same emphatic slowness as him, and adding that the dog in question was black and shaggy. Her hands sketched a large, rough circle in the air, presumably intended to represent the dog, but much too round because she couldn't draw dogs. To prevent misunderstandings, she proceeded to explain that you would, of course, have to prepare for the falling dog by putting down lots of rugs or, better still, a ball pool. Then, *kaboom*, the wet dog would fall from the sky and you could start to play with it – though it might be a good idea to dry it off with a hairdryer first, because wet dogs did smell a bit funny and it might have got rather cold flying through the air. And so on.

One hour and several outrageous answers later (all in response to completely standard questions), Nina was done, Dr Finkelbach was done in and we could finally go home.

In the lift, Nina asked in a whisper whether I thought Dr Finkelbach was a bit '*innervous*' – though he was, she added, very nice and she'd had fun thinking up such funny stories. I had a lump in my throat. I, too, was pretty done in after Nina's mind-blowing performance, and had to stop myself from giving this cheerful, unsuspecting four-year-old a serious lecture about how life isn't all fun and games; there are situations where it matters what you say and do, where mistakes have consequences, where you have to stick to the rules, and so on and so forth – the whole grown-up life's-a-serious-business spiel, which in fact I'd secretly been regarding as suspect for some time. And why didn't she just give the right answer and say *rain* – in fact, come to think of it, couldn't she have said something at least vaguely normal in response to all the other questions? We had, after all, had our little talk beforehand about not everyone understanding people who come, as Nina says of herself, '*a bit from another world*', where everything is different to planet Earth, and creatures like large flying mammals are entirely normal.

I took a very deep breath and inadvertently glimpsed a face in the lift mirror. It was a millisecond before I recognised myself in the tensed-up bloke glaring at me with an angry furrow in his brow. Then I caught Nina's eye and saw her trying to read my gaze. The lift doors opened; I took her little hand and we went and bought ice creams, although I didn't forget to wipe the chocolate from her face before we got home. Sweet stuff so soon before mealtimes was a private matter between Nina and me, not that I was under any illusion that my wife didn't notice.

* * *

Now, I read the letter in my lap. It was quite long, with the usual Greco-Latin mishmash of ridiculous names for the various physiological phenomena Nina was struggling with; nothing we didn't already know.

From the very beginning of her life, it was as if Nina had very carefully avoided doing what children are supposed to do. It had begun soon after she was born. At four months, your baby is supposed to have started smiling. There is scientific evidence that at around this time, babies develop a smile to show pleasure when they interact. If your baby fails to conform, you just have to wait. *She'll get there in the end.* Smiling is pretty important; it's the trick used by all professional babies to prevent their exhausted mothers from absconding – discreetly dumping their bags of shopping and packs of nappies on the pavement one evening and leaving the country. How could any woman forgive her baby for 53 sleepless nights in a row, sore nipples, bursting breasts, zero free time and zero independence, if she weren't rewarded with the occasional smile? No wonder smiling babies have been favoured by evolution. And of course, babies also do wonderful new things nearly every day – feats of seismic proportions, such as touching index finger to thumb so they can at last pluck the fluff from the carpet and put it in their mouths.

Nina began by doing nothing at all for eight months. She stared persistently into the distance with a very serious face, as if she had a lot of thinking to do. She barely reacted to being talked to or to any of the childish games that grown-ups go in for to get their offsprings' attention. There was no evidence of pleasure in interaction. I did sometimes suspect that she was intelligently observing us as we played out our lives, but I had no proof. When she wasn't staring into the distance, she was sleeping. She slept copiously – at least during the day, when carried around in a sling and hummed to at a moderate volume. Standing still or even clearing your throat led to such protracted protest that humming-walking was, on the whole, the more agreeable alternative. We didn't do much smiling, either. If you have a baby who never smiles, you automatically smile less yourself.

During this time, we were constantly taking Nina to be assessed. It always followed the same pattern: first the tests, then a week to wait for the results, trying to stay calm. Then more tests and more staying calm. Nina's developmental curves were phenomenal. Other children have beautiful sweeping curves with excellent mathematical functions that resemble upside-down ski jumps. The more quickly babies do things, the better. Nina's 'curves' were either straight horizontal lines, or looked as scrawled as the creatures she would later draw.

Despite this, there was hope: despite the rather dark prognoses we had received right after her birth, she had learned to walk and talk. All Nina's diagnoses stated that she had delayed development, especially in her motorics. This left a lot of space for hope and imagination. Things are neither broken nor missing, just delayed. So, with a bit of time…

And indeed, now, at nearly five years old, Nina was prepared to make compromises when she felt it was important. She had recognised, for example, that grown-ups find communication easier if you talk to them. Smiling was no longer a problem and she'd even overtaken me on that front. Therefore we clung to the notion that our life would eventually resume its course – that it would one day be more or less normal again; halfway normal, anyway, or maybe a quarter-way. The notion of normality is stubborn. It is, after all, what keeps everything moving. In theory, at least.

Even though the assessment with Dr Finkelbach had been startling in various ways, somehow I had still managed to put a positive spin on it. Maybe a psychologist would know what to do; maybe even therapy with animals, dolphins if available – that kind of thing. Or perhaps he'd resort to some bottom-line talk about accepting what was real and what wasn't.

I turned the pages of the letter, scanning it for anything new. These latest results were also described in ancient languages, and were shot through with outlandish expressions to outline a number of cognitive and behavioural abnormalities. In some areas, Nina's test results were right off the map. Even the well-meaning and creative evaluation of Dr Finkelbach couldn't square that. As for 90° rotated drawings of people who look like run-over aliens, with excess limbs in places never intended by nature – they're not quite the ticket either, if you're testing a subject for hand-eye coordination, visual processing capacity and cognitive processing speed. There also were some comments on Nina's apparent inability to clearly distinguish fiction and reality. A wet talking dog, for example, appealing though the idea may be, doesn't yield any points in such standardised tests, especially if it also happens to fly. In a medical report, wet flying dogs translated into serious questions about Nina's 'age-adequate life orientation', which might have serious implications for academic performance, future career, etc.

Maybe Dr Finkelbach used the word 'serious' in his report so often because of my own performance during the test session. Or maybe it was to show that Nina's situation was, in fact, serious. No matter how complicated the tables, graphs and text, his conclusions were simple. The black-and-white integrity of Finkelbach's letter carried three unmistakable messages:

1.   This is how it is.
2.   It is difficult.
3.   This is how it's going to stay.

*Yes, your life is going to look as way-out in the future as it has done for the last four years, since Nina entered your lives. Possibly even more so. In fact, this is probably only the tip of the iceberg. Yours sincerely, etc.*

I continued to browse through the letter numbly while Vera drank her tea and waited. The more I read, the more it became evident that Nina had almost nothing in common with the image that a paediatric psychologist, teacher, doctor or educational policymaker might have of a well-balanced child. Her memorable performance in Finkelbach's test was light years away from the statistical average expected of children her age, and the wonderful world inside her head was a kind of parallel universe that didn't conform to any recognised psychological pattern. And yet Nina herself seemed to feel that this was just fine. She regularly behaved as if she were a stubborn extraterrestrial pensioner on holiday.

As far as I could judge, for example, Nina was aware that hands are, on the whole, attached to arms and equipped with approximately five fingers. But she seemed to regard such a factual depiction of reality as overly pedantic – quite apart from her genuine physical problems, which began with her inability to hold a pencil properly. Sometimes it was very difficult to tell whether she did things on purpose, because in everyday life she blithely failed to stick to a single rule. In a hypothetical football match, Nina would cause several scandals within the first five minutes just by doing her thing, but sending her off would mean missing a weird and wonderful game. Ever since this little girl had started lurching determinedly through my carefully planned life like a combination of Charlie Chaplin and Pinocchio, the future seemed guaranteed to take a completely different course.

I finished reading the report and exchanged a wistful smile with my wife. I knew Vera was right. We didn't have the faintest idea where we were headed with our eldest child, but I had to reluctantly acknowledge that an international career was no longer viable. I wasn't going to be taking up that job in Cape Town and holding out for a professorship. You don't do that kind of job part-time. It was also becoming obvious that I couldn't continue to travel the world 30 weeks a year on consultant assignments for the UN, leaving Vera and the kids at home. For the egocentric workaholic in me, the guy who had glared at his reflection in the lift, it briefly felt like the end of all my dreams. I had so carefully put together the jigsaw of my life, and now it seemed as if I had chosen the wrong pieces. I would have to start again from the beginning, and do it differently.

While I was digesting the devastating implications, Nina came into the room and blithely curled up on Vera's lap.

'Are you having an important meeting?' she asked, and chuckled.

I had to smile. Nothing would mess with Nina's irresistible *joie de vivre*, her unassailable humour or the innocent power of her dreams.

For a while none of us said anything. Vera looked me straight in the eye and waited.

'Now, did you know that some dogs can fly?' I said.

# NO STRESSTIC

BONN (50°44'N, 7°5'E)
RHINELAND, GERMANY

MY SHORT-TERM SOLUTION WAS TO TAKE 20 DAYS' annual leave. Four weeks off work is not that much if you intend to change your whole life. In the institute where I worked, however, 20 days away from your desk amounted to an absurd, potentially business-damaging holiday. The only reason they let me get away with it was because, for the first time, I had started talking about our situation at home in more detail. Naturally, I had promised to attend some important appointments and (of course) work on an urgent manuscript, and I had announced that (as usual) I would always be contactable. If I had known what to expect when juggling work queries and time with Nina, I might not have made quite such a commitment.

During this time off I did a lot of things I had never done before. One day, I found myself alone in a posh shop that sold all kinds of exotic vehicles for children. It smelled like a car dealer's showroom.

'Goes like a rocket,' the salesman said, lovingly stroking the highly polished dark red paintwork. I looked hesitantly at the shiny velocipede. There was no denying it was handsome.

'Our best model by far,' he went on excitedly. 'The most elegant you'll get for your money. The Xrt 3 GIGA is, you might say, the *connoisseur's choice.'* He wiggled his index and middle fingers up and down.

I nodded appreciatively and he flashed me a seductive smile. He knew what he was doing. All the same, though, he still hadn't got me quite where he wanted me. I gave the saddle an undecided pat, feeling the *bionic water-repellent surface* that wouldn't get wet, no matter what fell from the sky.

'Our signal feature – are you ready?' He pushed the button on the electronic bell and the wail of a police siren filled the shop, making the people around us jump. 'State of the art! And impossible to miss. Everyone'll know about it when this little tearaway comes whizzing along.' He looked about apologetically and added that there were quieter settings if I wanted.

'Do you think it might be possible to have another brake put on?' I asked.

He gave me a baffled look. 'What do you mean?'

'Could you put a brake on the handlebars? In case the little tearaway happened to be whizzing along too fast – downhill, say?'

The man gave me a doubtful look. 'You brake with your feet, by pressing down on the pedals.'

I explained that this might be asking too much of the tearaway in question. The salesman reached for his phone and said he needed to contact the workshop about special orders like that; if I would just bear with him...

Really the tricycle was too challenging for Nina. And it was not, admittedly, the first time we were buying something without knowing whether she'd ever be able to use it – as if the mere fact of buying it might somehow increase her chances of success. It's a poignant feeling, watching things pile up in the cellar still in their original packaging. Of course, Nina was well past the age when other children were breaking world tricycle records daily, but she was still far from being able to handle such a speedy vehicle. All the same, I couldn't wait to see her careering down our street on it. I pictured myself cheering her on: what a milestone! Vera and I were very keen on the idea that everything would sort itself out some day – we clung to it like a lifebelt.

I was told that for a hefty surcharge, the in-house mechanic could install the additional brake. If I was in a rush, they could have it ready by Saturday afternoon.

'No, next week will be fine,' I said. 'So, what else can it do?'

I wanted to reassure myself that I hadn't missed anything. The Renault 5 I bought when I left school hadn't cost much more than this trike, and that had included welding work on the undercarriage.

'Basically everything,' he said. 'It's an all-terrain vehicle.' He cleared his throat and I saw a fervent flash in his eyes, as he wondered whether I'd grasped the significance of his words. 'It runs on tarmac, but it can also be ridden on sand or coarse gravel and in all weather conditions. The wheels are solid rubber, so it never has any trouble gripping. And here' – he solemnly tapped the back axle – 'you have exclusively high-end ball bearings. They were developed for space travel, so there's virtually no mechanical friction loss.' Then he winked and said, 'The only place you're maybe best not riding it is on the motorway.'

I swallowed. The good man, carried away with his salesmanly high spirits, had unwittingly touched a sore point; because life with Nina really did feel like heading down the motorway on a tricycle. Nina was, as she put it, *swow*. Unbelievably *swow*. Beside her humour and rampant imagination, *swowness* was probably her most striking feature. She did everything in her own time – and that could be a very long time indeed. Her generally dismissive attitude to the unnecessarily hectic nature of grown-up life did not change, no matter how carefully I tried to explain my adult perspective. Far from it: the more she thought about this, the more sure she seemed to become. It was sensational. She celebrated every precious moment of life, and there were so many of them. Half a bread roll topped with salami and four slices of cucumber was consumed in 19 minutes. In theory, of course, she could have just got on with eating it. Instead, she made a kind of ceremony out of the process, like a Michelin-starred chef deconstructing a menu designed by his greatest mentor. She gazed at the roll for a long time. Gave a little introductory talk. Tried a first bite. *Oh. It's fallen down.* Volunteered further impressions. Separated the various layers. Tasted each in turn. Reassembled the layers in the reverse order. *Sticks to the plate.* Launched into a digression on the subject. Tried biting into the sandwich from the other side. Carefully put some special part of it aside to save for later. And so on.

The 100-metre walk to the organic grocer's took us 25 minutes – one way. I made a point of walking on the side of the road that was not inhabited by *the poor lonely dog* that lived there. But Nina seemed to be personally acquainted with every bloody woodlouse on our street. Putting on her shoes (the ones with Velcro): four minutes. Per shoe.

I had once cautiously asked the neurologist how I could best imagine what it meant to have 'severely impaired fine motor skills' – and why my life these days seemed to proceed in slow motion. He said, 'If you want to know how it feels for your daughter, just try tying your shoes with chopsticks and with a 15kg weight on each wrist. Then try to be as fast as possible.'

Usually, Nina was immensely patient with herself; I have no idea where she got her tolerance for frustration – certainly not from me. Stand up, fall down. Stand up, fall down. I once timed how long she could go without losing her patience in situations where I would have been cursing almost immediately. Tying her shoelaces, she held out for nearly four minutes before the dam wall finally broke and she began to hurl the worst abuse she could muster at the *pleetly noying* shoes.

Often, I wasn't sure whether she stretched time to its limits because she really couldn't do things faster, or because she'd just decided to do things her way – here, in the middle of *my* life. But actually, of course, she was right: those 19 minutes it took her to eat that bread and salami belonged to *her*, not me, didn't they?

'It isn't easy for you, is it?' she asked me on one of these slow-motion afternoons, when I had an urgent appointment, six minutes ago. Nina made my life look like Dalí's melting watches. She must have caught me holding my breath again, my lips pressed tightly together, as I stood beside her while she took half an eternity to put on one sock. That was something I'd caught myself doing a lot during these 20 days – forgetting to breathe out under the sheer pressure of time. Her hands suddenly abandoned the helpless tugging; she looked up at me and smiled soothingly at her impatient parent. 'No stresstic,' she said.

We were so lucky that our little girl was so patient with us. Even so, it seems there is no place in ordinary life for spectacular *swowness*, especially if you're bent on driving on the motorway. (Everyone else does, after all.) One solution to the difficulty of riding a tricycle down the motorway is, of course, to try to accelerate to a normal speed – as if it weren't a tricycle at all. If, like me, you've spent all your life in the fast lane, that seems only natural. My UN background had trained me to operate under the constant pressure of time, but from the very first day of trying to reconcile a hectic daily life with a profoundly relaxed child, I was a failure. During my 20 days off, I arrived late for several business appointments. Some of my colleagues found it hard to understand. For the first time since high school, I was criticised for being late. Me, the time-management pro! I was caught between Nina on the one hand, dreaming her way through the day with unconcerned *swowness*, and the rush of day-to-day trivia on the other.

Even though I had always been aware of Nina being much slower than other kids, I seriously underestimated the consequences that professional *swowness* can have for a daily life that is otherwise run by people who think in terms of efficiency and pragmatism. This was one of the things that Vera had been trying to tell me for years. When I spent time with Nina, it was mostly at the weekend, during holidays, in exceptional circumstances where we had some time to spare. But under normal conditions – that is, with hardly any time for anything – the situation was 'serious', as Dr Finkelbach had termed it.

When directors of Hollywood tearjerkers want to show us that a character has reached a point where he or she is no longer in control of his or her life, they invariably resort to a particular analogy. I recall variations on this scene with Dustin Hoffman, Tom Hanks, Jennifer Aniston (of course) and Ben Stiller. In the first shot, we see the character who's gradually losing his grip (let's say it's a man) sitting in his car in a traffic jam. This guy has been working his way through a long to-do list, but now he's stuck in traffic. (This works best in New York City, because there's something particularly impressive about a traffic jam full of yellow taxis.) He drums on the steering wheel with a worried look on his face. He runs his hand nervously through his hair. He sighs. Cut to a small, cute child, sitting all by herself (let's say it's a girl) on the edge of a broad flight of steps outside a big, brightly painted school building. The huge schoolyard is deserted. The child has drawn up her knees and wrapped her arms around them and is gazing gloomily at her shoes. Sometimes we cut back and forth between the two scenes. The neglected kid. The frantic dad. I constantly felt like that man.

*   *   *

When I fetched the new tricycle out of the cellar a few days later, after Nina had rigorously rejected it a couple of times, she beamed at me. I hadn't been expecting that. Well, I thought, that's something. A small step forwards.

But then: 'You're riding it today,' she said.

'Oh, come on, it doesn't matter if it doesn't work out,' I said. 'We'll just give it a go – no stresstic!' I pushed the tricycle to and fro a few times with a flourish, to tempt her. The siren battery seemed to have given up the ghost.

'No, *you*,' she said.

I recognised that tone. It meant that if I wanted to get anywhere, I was going to have to give in to some of Nina's demands. So I manoeuvred myself onto the little saddle, which was pretty uncomfortable, and tried to get my feet on the pedals. If I splayed my legs like a frog, I could just about fit the sides of my shoes on them. At least there was no one else around on our street to witness me. I started to pedal. No need for the brake, at least.

'You see,' I said. 'Like this.'

Nina nodded encouragement.

*Don't give up*, I told myself, putting my back into it. Nina staggered along beside me; children like her walk like sailors who have lingered too long in the harbour pub. For a while we moved along the street in silence. What a moment: a small, drunk child holding hands with a six-foot-tall frog on a dark red tricycle. My feet had begun to ache, but I kept pedalling.

'I like it when you ride,' Nina said.

'Because I look so funny?'

'No, because you cannot run away. We are so nice and *swow*. Then we have a lot of time.'

That night I wrote in my journal: *The slower you are, the more time you have.* Oh, I was learning a lot from Nina's lectures these days. But the biggest lecture of all was yet to come.

When I was putting Nina to bed a few days later, she followed up my enthusiastic reading of Story Number One with the routine reminder that good dads always read more than one bedtime story.

I answered truthfully that I had a lot to do and could only spare another ten minutes. It was already 8:23pm according to the Piaget, and my to-do list was – to put it optimistically – only half-completed. Apart from anything else, I had the deadline for that UNESCO manuscript the following day.

'Ten minutes? Ten minutes for three stories? You must be a bit confused,' Nina chirped from deep within a pile of pillows. Two arms emerged and pulled at my neck. 'Oh, Daddy, I wish we had a million minutes. Just for all the really nice things, you know?' She squeezed my face between her hands so that I looked like a cleaner fish sucking at the side of an aquarium. 'A million minutes. Tomorrow you can tell me a million-minute story, all right? And today you can finish doing your *stresstic*, OK?'

There can't be many things as unnerving as being reminded of your original dreams by your own children. It must have been Finkelbach's letter and Nina's million-minute idea coming back to back that did it; some psychological threshold was crossed. At any rate, it was at that precise moment that it hit me, right there in Nina's room. A crack appeared in my daily 1,440-minute routine. I did the calculation in my journal later, before starting on the UNESCO manuscript:

The crack ran right through the core of my life – through a pretty skewed concept of work-life balance, through normal career goals, through the image of a healthy family, of fatherhood, partnership, through ideas of what it means to be rich and happy, and how a day-to-day life should actually look. More than anything, though, the crack ran through the idea that it was perfectly natural to have time for everything except the things that mattered most.

Do you remember the scene in *The Truman Show* where Truman Burbank, the unwitting lead actor in a live TV show, is sailing into the sun on an apparently endless ocean, when he suddenly crashes into the sky-blue plasterboard backdrop he had always thought to be the horizon? It's a fundamental, irreversible moment – and something similar had just happened to me. Nina's question that evening had forced me to admit that there was a different world behind the backdrop of my ordinary day-to-day routine, and I couldn't pretend I wasn't interested any more. Just as there's no persuading Burbank that there's nothing on the other side of that fake sky, it was impossible for me to get those million minutes out of my head – even without the almost systematic persistence with which Nina returned to the subject in the weeks that followed.

Finkelbach's letter had certainly triggered a lot of hairline cracks. Then there was the turmoil of feeling torn between too many demands, trying to act as though everything was under control, while Nina continued to innocently question everything that I had thought was completely normal. No surprise that her revolutionary idea hit a nerve.

*A million minutes. Just for all the really nice things.*

Maybe that was the first piece of the new jigsaw that I was supposed to build?

# TIME TRAVELLERS

'YOU ARE GOING TO DO *WHAT?!*'

For a while, with a strong emphasis on the *what*, this flabbergasted reaction came top whenever I mentioned our idea of a lovely two-year journey through some of the more remote places on earth (six times). There was also the ironic, 'Yes, sure...' (five times), followed by, 'And I'm the Emperor of China' (three times). Our announcement was a kind of secret test balloon to figure out how our family and friends would respond and whether, in our growing enthusiasm, we had overlooked any weighty arguments. Mostly, people were well intentioned; after all, until recently my career had played a vital part in our life planning, and some friends only knew me as a workaholic. From a medical point of view, Nina's history was not exactly a recommendation. Simon was just a few months old. We were not millionaires, not if you measured wealth in money. It seemed fantastical that we would leave secure careers, take off and travel around the world.

What we'd actually do was not self-evident, as I pretended. A movie hero would have had a plan at his fingertips. (That hero wouldn't have waited for years before taking action in the first place, which was a somewhat bitter insight.) Although I liked to give the impression that I had a clear vision, I had felt pretty clueless since Nina's request. As much as the idea of having time was appealing, what do you do with a million minutes?

My bewilderment was, surely, an exclusively adult preserve. I would have liked to ask my friend Anna Amsel about it. (It was a running gag between us that I never called her Anna, always Anna Amsel or even Dr Amsel.) Anna Amsel was a psychotherapist – purely out of curiosity, she always said. I would have liked to ask her whether there is an official psychological term for people who don't know what to do with their time: perhaps MAID, for Massive Adult Imagination Deficit. But MAID is hardly a surprising concept. If you rarely have any spare time, you don't have much need for imagination. If, say, you have approximately 135 minutes' free time every Thursday after work, between about 7 and 9:15pm, the question of how to fill that time more or less decides itself. You might have to choose between going to the gym, streaming a TV series, reading or doing something with your partner. Or, of course, you could cook, or simply glance at your to-do list to refresh and reload the MAID. Either way, you've no need to worry about ideas. It's the same if you go on a fortnight's holiday. There, too, it's clear from the outset what you can and can't do. Even highly optimised Japanese tour groups don't manage more than six European capitals in a fortnight.

I think MAID is triggered by those to-do lists. To-do lists are the devil's work: they convert time, transforming your lovely life into little ticks next to petty trivia. Before you know where you are, a quarter of an hour has metamorphosed into the purchase of 25 50-litre grey bin liners. And 126 minutes have transformed into changing your tyres. Almost a thousand minutes vanish before you can finally put that little tick next to the words *tax return*. How time flies. *Tempus fugit, nihil manet.*

Our life, if you thought of it as time, was running away before our eyes, leaving nothing behind. My to-do lists had an outrageous habit of growing as I was working my way through them. One morning, I had abused my precious journal in order to get so-urgent things out of my head. The items at the top of the list read:

Reply to Education Office email
Appointment – Ms Schengen!
Ring bank (number?)
Liability certifcate
Collect jacket from dry cleaner
Toilet paper, pepper, oranges, mineral water

To my mind, to-do lists represent the dictatorship of the *endlessly urgent*. Each little particle of the endlessly urgent has its individual legitimacy; you can't avoid going to the dentist, for example. The endlessly urgent never stops, and it can pulverise a lifetime – but it doesn't always match the *important*. (Obviously, basic needs like eating, drinking and sleeping are urgent *and* important.) Nevertheless, many of the important things that matter don't even feature on our to-do lists. I really ought to have written my lists on pre-printed forms headed with the words *TIME WITH THE KIDS* in 32-point alongside the other things that really mattered. When you think about it, it's weird that in Germany you have to apply for parental leave. If you forget to send off the application, does this mean that you're a parent with no time, or not a parent at all?

At some stage I must have surrendered to the endlessly urgent without noticing. I'd spent so long just working my way down my to-do lists, it was no surprise that it took a while to realise what was going on in my family. Unlike me, they weren't suffering from MAID.

One evening, before Nina's million-minutes suggestion, Vera and I had been watching a quiz show. A contestant said that if he won the jackpot, he'd start by going on a 'big trip'. It's a popular goal. Watch enough quiz shows and you'll notice that eight out of ten contestants dream of doing just that.

'These long journeys,' Vera sighed, as she went into the kitchen to find a bottle of our favourite wine. She began to wallow in memories of the months we had once spent backpacking around Latin America. 'That was such a beautiful time, do you remember?'

'It was,' I agreed, but I didn't get the hint.

I'm not sure when I finally realised that Nina, Vera and even baby Simon were busy forging a strategic alliance.

One afternoon I tiptoed into the children's room. Nina was standing by her little brother's cot, haranguing him in urgent tones. 'Really! Do you understand, Mr Simon?' (She always called him that.) 'A whole million! You can get really far with a million minutes.'

The floorboards creaked under my feet and Nina looked over, immediately falling silent. (What had she meant by 'far'?) Mr Simon smiled an enthusiastic, toothless smile of agreement. He had no idea what he was letting himself in for.

The moment when it really clicked in my head was one of those evenings during which Vera tried to explain a number of very exotic and elaborate therapeutic measures that we were supposed to adopt with Nina to promote her sensomotorical skills. Only now did I begin to understand how my wife had spent the last year while I was so busy saving the endemic epiphytic orchid flora in semi-degraded neotropical mountain rainforests in the Chocó department of Colombia.

Earlier that day, Vera had called to ask me to buy 6.5kg of peas on my way home. No, dry peas. No, the colour would not matter. Yes, she would explain later what they were for. I had to visit three different shops to accomplish my mission. The owner of the Turkish corner shop nodded approvingly as I shovelled the last three kilos into a bag. The last 50 times I had visited his shop I had bought junk food.

It seemed that the peas were for a sensomotorically stimulating bath for Nina. While Vera placed the peas and the child into a big bucket she explained that, 'ideally', you would use sand. On a beach, for example. But if you didn't have a beach, 6.5kg of dried peas would be fine. Water was excellent as well, she said. 'Ideally', Nina would frequently bathe in the ocean. The sound of the waves, and all that – perfect. But if no ocean was available, a bathtub offered a makeshift stop-gap. When she started to explain that you could spend

20 minutes on a full-body blow-dry with a hairdryer to recreate the warm wind of a tropical island, I asked her outright:

'Are you trying to tell me something?'

'No, not at all,' she claimed.

But she had a huge smile on her face when she asked me to prepare a giant bowl of warm water containing about four litres of bath foam for Nina to experiment with (another of the therapeutic measures that had been recommended).

Finally, I understood.

Even better: I did not have to be a hero to do what so clearly needed to be done. There it was, the solution, right in front of me; and I had the best motive in the world!

Since Nina's birth, it had gradually become clear that the more time we devoted to her, the more she thrived. When she was about six months old we flew to South Africa, where I was supposed to give a talk and work on a project at the country's National Biodiversity Institute. In my typical career guy's mindset, it was legitimate to combine pleasure with pragmatism…

Unexpectedly, that first trip away with Nina turned out to be highly beneficial for her. In fact, whenever we went on holiday, she blossomed. During a trip to Namibia she smiled for the first time (she must have liked the bumpy drive on the washboard tracks). She was almost nine months old by then, but for a while that smile remained a one-off and I began to wonder if I'd dreamt it. But then she began to smile more and more. At the time, I thought it a coincidence. Then, on a campsite in southern France, Nina started to talk. It came out of the blue after three days of high fever. Unable to pull herself along or crawl – she still spent most of her time lying on her back – she began to grope her way forward verbally. Within a few months, her vocabulary had exploded. She sent out small, fragile sentences, fathoming the world like an echo sounder. While Nina was immobile in our apartment, she would often ask me to fetch objects of interest so I could explain them to her. What felt like an eternity later, Nina waited until the first day of a holiday on Mallorca to stand up for the first time. By then she was two – and there she was, suddenly, leaning against my leg, the way she would propel herself for the next few years. It was during a visit to Great Auntie Marlie's in Berlin that she took her first steps.

Everything momentous always happened to Nina when we were on holiday. Was this because we had more time together when we were away?

It seems to me that travelling is an effective antidote to to-do lists, as it makes them completely redundant. What is there to tick off when you're sitting by your tent in the Fish River Canyon? Friends were always asking what Nina could do and since when. More and more, our replies were in the form of place names rather than dates. She'd been able to catch a ball since Whitby, told her first joke in Ameland, learned to swing in Aix-en-Provence. Whenever we went anywhere, we could be sure that something wonderful would happen.

*   *   *

Without my severe case of MAID, I would probably have been less *swow* to connect the pieces of the jigsaw. But even I managed it eventually. This was the equation:

A theoretical million minutes +
a completely unrealistic journey +
the best motive in the world =
a once-in-a-lifetime combination!

That evening, after sourcing about 1,367 peas which Nina had joyfully and carefully distributed throughout our entire flat while singing a song about Cinderella, something shifted in my heart: this was not the end of my dreams. It was actually the beginning. The four of us were about to become time travellers.

Before I went to sleep, I noted in my journal: How far is a million minutes?

# DOWNSIZING

BONN (50° 44' N, 7° 5' E)
RHINELAND, GERMANY

I'D HAD AN EXCITING CAREER, BUT IT WAS ACTUALLY most spectacular at its finale.

Slamming on the brakes the way I did is regarded as unusual behaviour, especially when you've been going at full throttle. I had hundreds of personal contacts, long-term collaborative projects all over the world, ongoing publications, exciting ideas for research and a journal packed full of appointments and flight bookings for months into the future. When I changed direction so dramatically, I was on the phone for days, just talking to my project partners, many of whom had become friends.

It feels strange to saw off the branch you're sitting on – especially when people keep trying to wrestle the saw out of your hands. I don't know how many people asked me whether I was *sure*. It made me feel unsure, to say the least. Some people, I could tell, thought I was nuts. And what about all the collaborative projects? I couldn't just abandon them. Couldn't my better half take care of *that*? But the thing was, I told them, *that* happens to be my daughter. Others made impulsive remarks like, 'Wolf, you're screwing up your entire future.' It wasn't easy, taking those comments from friends. Did they really think I had a choice?

My boss, an old-school patriarch who had devoted his entire life to science, tried, rather helplessly, to make things easier for me. He handed me my more-than-generous testimonial across his enormous laden desk and announced, 'Come back when things have sorted themselves out.'

I looked at him. Our gazes wandered over the pile of books between us. We both knew how unlikely it was that I would ever return. The clock was always ticking in that world. People in the fast lane need an extremely good reason to take time off. Spending your afternoons swinging coloured cloths to and fro in front of an unamused child as part of some sophisticated therapy, or bathing the same (rather more cheerful) child in dried peas and marbles doesn't appear to constitute an extremely good reason. From a human resources perspective, a dangerous and even inexcusable void had suddenly appeared in my previously immaculate CV.

*   *   *

The frequently asked questions that follow 'You-are-going-to-do-what?' are all about money. 'Did you win the lottery?' 'So where have you got the money from?' This, too, was one of my concerns. We didn't own a property and had barely any savings. Only six months ago we had taken out a loan to buy some new furniture, a car and the materials to build a carport (basically an open garage) next to our rented apartment. Quitting my relatively new and secure well-paid job wasn't exactly a promising method of financing two years of travelling, during which neither Vera nor I would be generating an income. Actually, when you consider how modern society creates a chain of value, it looked like we were making a big error. I drew an arrow diagram in my journal to illustrate this another way (I'm a scientist, I can't help it):

The great value-added chain

0.00014 % life

Some mental tricks convert life-time into disposable time (or how long we have to live)

00:60

60 min

Work transforms time into money

$20.00 net

Shopping transforms money into a something

'New elegant plastic floral print phone case 37g'

Owning a something creates, if everything goes really well, positive feelings

Hmm...hard to say how many positive feelings that phone case generates, even if it is pretty snazzy.

I think we act as if the time we have on earth, or our lives, are a form of abstract currency. We spend this time as if we are immortal. It's true that many people, even in 21st-century Europe, don't have any choice: they have to devote at least half their lives to earning money just to ensure their basic needs are met – a roof over their heads, enough to eat and so on.

It's mind-blowing what happens when you try to bypass this value chain and just live your life directly, before converting it into time spent earning money to purchase assets. It isn't easy. As soon as you stop, you run into considerable difficulties: wage loss, consumption squeeze, pension cuts. No small matters. In the course of preparing for our trip, I felt as if I had to refinance my own lifetime. *Good morning, I would like a million minutes of my life, please. Oh? I have to ransom myself first...?*

\* \* \*

The refinancing of our lives had begun with Nina's million-minute idea, which I thought of as introducing a crucial and irreversible currency reform. I was shifting from thinking in terms of money and professional achievements to thinking in terms of time. In my journal, I scribbled: how many minutes could I buy for €250? How many euros do a million minutes cost? Or to be more precise: how much more expensive is a million-minute journey compared to a million minutes of normal life? That was the big question.

Our trip became more tangible one sunny afternoon in our sitting room. Vera was researching while I was paying bills. After a while, she poked me in the side and smiled.

'Look. Maybe all we need to do is not buy a car.' She'd found a website with some very fine-looking specimens.

'Eh?' I stared at her blankly.

'I've been looking into this,' she said, 'and I've decided I'd really like to not buy a Volkswagen Passat. This silver metallic Passat Comfortline Variant, for example. Just the depreciation in the first year is stupendous! Equivalent to about two months' world travel for all the family, including flights.' She winked at me. 'So if we don't buy the Passat, that would give us at least several hundred thousand minutes for all the family to gad around the tropics.'

Vera looked at me. She seemed to expect a response, but I couldn't quite share her enthusiasm.

'To be honest...' I said.

She tried again. 'Don't buy it, save it?' She raised her eyebrows.

I began to see what she was getting at.

'And if we decide not to take added luxury features such as the electronic Driver Alert System to avoid tiredness-related issues or the multifunction steering wheel or the... let's have a look... Active Info Display, that would take us to 16 months.'

'We could do without heated wing mirrors too,' I suggested.

'Yes, excellent, we don't need those either.'

'And I could build a non-carport.' I was getting into this now.

'Great idea! No car, plus the loan money for the non-carport and the non-furniture – that adds up to nearly a million minutes! Plus it would give us added luxury features – more time for children, reading, hobbies, beach activities... and getting enough sleep, the number one system for avoiding tiredness-related issues.'

'Not bad,' I said appreciatively.

I jotted a few thoughts down in the form of an equation:

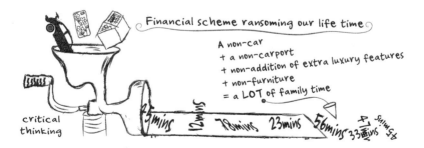

Our refinancing plans were coming on in leaps and bounds. Instead of spending our time raising the money to pay for a car and all that, we would not buy these things and generate the time instead. When we got back from our trip, we'd still have to find the rest of the repayments, but... that was a million minutes away. In retrospect, there was something interesting about our carport plans. I remembered the conversations we had had with friends. Should we build it from scratch? Use timber or brick? Double or single? But nobody had *ever* said 'You are going to do what?' Using a significant portion of our lifetime's earnings to build a house for a car was seen as fine. Using the same money to spend some fantastic time with your loved ones was, on the other hand, very strange.

There was another way to break the value-added chain. Even if you had already converted quite a proportion of your lifetime into assets, it wasn't too late to reverse this. Now we could help finance our million-minute trip by selling the possessions we no longer needed. Sitting in our flat surrounded by all our furniture, books, accessories, souvenirs and household objects – not to mention the things that didn't seem to fit into any category – I considered that nobody on a journey of a million minutes would choose to accumulate baggage. In life, though – on the great big 42-million-minute journey – it seemed to be the other way round. Our flat in Bonn was chock-a-block with life's baggage. Like our third tea service (an heirloom). The teak knife block (a Christmas present from friends). The eclectic collection of tea light holders along the windowsills. Ancient souvenirs cast adrift from their histories. Clothes nobody wore. Unread books and papers in piles next to the bookshelves because I didn't know what to do with them. You get to the point where you've accumulated so much stuff that you have to start putting up cupboards. Then you need a larger flat to accommodate all the cupboards. I had CDs in duplicate, broken things I'd long ago replaced and things I thought might one day turn out to be useful. I once went through our cutlery drawer and counted 25 palette knives. I didn't even know where most of them had come from. Might it not be a good idea to use the coming journey as an excuse to jettison some of this ballast? The airline's non-negotiable baggage limit for the four of us was 69kg. The belongings we would travel with were allowed to add up to about a third of our total family weight. Excess baggage can cost up to €80 per kilo, depending on the airline's rules. That really does force you to make a complete reappraisal: hairdryer 300g, plus radio 2kg, plus a couple of books equals €250. Multiplied by the many flights that we would take.

The first three decisions are easy when you're downsizing. One, get rid of anything you have more than one of. Two, hang onto sentimental items, like old photo albums. Three, don't throw out anything useful. No point in chucking the potato peeler or the Swiss Army knife. But where do you go from there?

Dennis Niebel – 'We clear houses of any size' – was a pro. The van that drew up outside our house was buttercup yellow, but the man who got out was dressed elegantly in black.

'My condolences,' he said, shaking my hand with a look of conscientious sadness.

'We're all still alive,' I said with a smile. 'I'm just trying to part with a few things.'

'Ah, downsizing. Good decision.'

His hand fluttered on my shoulder. Good for him, because downsizers like me upsized his business, or good for me? I took him round the flat, pointing out what I could imagine parting with. First, my suits.

'Oh no… tailor-made… and no removable armpit pads?' he asked, with a look of distress. 'Off-the-rack products without workers' sweat' would eventually sell, as he put it. But my suits were worthless, of course. An old Zeiss Ikon camera with a fold-out concertina lens fetched €80 and a bit of space in my cupboard. A neighbour who was no longer alive had given it to me when I was 14 and I'd carried it through my life ever since, without ever using it.

To my great surprise, Mr Niebel ignored the shiny Xrt 3 GIGA tricycle which was standing in our corridor. When I drew his attention to it, he explained that in that price category, people would not buy second-hand – because of potential damage to the paintwork, for example. My voice sounded unintentionally defiant when I replied that there must be children who would be pleased to play with such a fancy tricycle, despite minor cosmetic defects. In a professional tone, which reminded me of my conversations with Anna Amsel, Mr Niebel explained that the children's perspective was neither here nor there. In this price category, it was simply a very important part of the parents' experience that the device was both new and expensive.

I noted in my journal three tips for downsizing:

1. If you want to know a thing's real value before you buy it, list it on eBay.
2. If you want to establish whether others share your view that a thing is great, try lending it to someone for a million minutes.
3. And if you still want that thing, calculate what it will cost as hold baggage.

My watches were next. There was a neat symbolism to converting watches into money to buy minutes for our journey. Dennis Niebel's eyes narrowed in suspicion. Was that a replica from Asia?

No, it was duty-free from London. Complete with receipt.

My appointment with Dennis went quickly, and the prices offered were low. It was a painful business. My Piaget watch would give us a few thousand minutes travelling the world, which was brilliant. But giving it up left me feeling empty.

Books? I showed Dennis my mini-library – about 1,500 books I had once been proud of. He went up to the shelves and sniffed them.

'Ah, books without smoker's lung. Very good.'

His eyes wandered up and down the spines. 'Now then… We don't usually take specialist literature. No one wants academic stuff, you know. Fiction's all right. Buy it by weight – €5 per kilo. Should add up to quite a tidy sum, I'd say, looking at these shelves.'

This was pretty much how I'd imagined the back-to-front value chain: 492 pages of Vargas Llosa's *The Way to Paradise* would be converted into 624g, which would be turned into money (€3.12), which would be turned into travel mileage, which would be converted into about 44 minutes. And those 44 minutes would come to 0.004% of a million minutes of unforgettable, lovely life – though, off the top of my head, I couldn't come up with a unit of measure. Maybe QTs – quality times? The modern notion of quality time was another trick I had used as the Curitiba high-flyer to gloss over my time poverty. When you get home in the evening after a whole day without seeing your child and have only ten minutes before she goes to bed, it sounds better if you call those ten minutes *quality time* – though if you think about it only a little too long, you begin to wonder what the opposite of quality time is: all those hours and hours that make up the rest of our lives. You wonder, too, why we see nothing strange in dedicating most of our lives to the nameless opposite of quality time. Still, those few QTs would be a beginning. One QT would be the length of a moment multiplied by the percentage spent doing what we really wanted to do. Maybe the million minutes ahead of us would contain more QTs than I had experienced in the whole of the last 15 years. In that case, there could be no harm in converting a few kilos of my possessions.

Dennis tore me out of my thoughts. 'That all right with you?'

The man was worth every cent he was going to make out of me. We decided to go for large-scale clearance.

'The whole hog, eh?' Dennis said, nodding enthusiastically, and dashed out to fetch some cardboard boxes.

\* \* \*

I stood on a chair, handing him books. García Márquez, *Love in the Time of Cholera*. I thought of Florentino, waiting over half a century, living a kind of surrogate life. Kundera, *The Unbearable Lightness of Being*. I thought of poor Franz standing on the street, watching the removal men. Prolific authors like these were valuable, and there was also a sizeable bonus for complete works, which I passed to Dennis balanced between my hands in small stacks.

*The Little Prince*. I hesitated. One of my favourites. I thought of all the stories: the strange rose, the elephant inside the snake, the little fox… I stopped in my tracks.

'Er, hang on, could I have that one back?'

Dennis generously fished the book out of the box. 'Can be hard, I know,' he said cheerfully.

I turned it over in my hand. On the cover, the little prince was smiling. *The essential is invisible to the eyes.* I returned the book to Dennis, this time paying close attention as it passed from my hand to his.

Nothing happened. The stories were all there still. The king who orders the sun to set, the volcanoes that need constant sweeping, the little prince's encounters with the geographer and the vain man, the snake in the desert. It was all there – deep inside me.

Quick, onto the next book. *The Bad Girl* by Vargas Llosa. This was a story that had hit me hard. I handed it to Dennis. Once again: it was all there. I still couldn't recall Otilia's cool cruelty without choking up. I reached for Vargas Llosa's other books. Dennis gave me an encouraging nod.

What did I have to lose? What do you lose when you give away a book whose stories have been there with you all your life? Had I discovered a paradoxical truth – that the more something *means* to you, the easier it is to give up the material part of it? Is that why it had been so painful to lose the Piaget, because, unlike the books, my expensive watch meant nothing to me, and therefore had left no trace of itself? There, I thought, was an insight I could carry through life without weighing myself down: things it hurts to lose are of no real significance, whereas things of real significance can't ever be lost.

\* \* \*

Some decisions don't seem easy at first. Not long ago, I was a man who gave speeches at important conferences, stayed in prestigious hotels, enjoyed a very high standard of living and had a job with status. Now, I was unemployed, pedalling on a children's tricycle through an otherwise quite empty flat. I hardly possessed any furniture, and instead had a rather large loan for this non-furniture. (We'd leave just enough money behind for a million minutes' worth of loan repayments, and worry about the rest of the loan when we got back.) You could even say that I owned a non-car (and a non-carport).

However, I was beginning to see the situation quite differently. I saved four boxes of my most personal items and stowed them with my mother; I had 1,500 books in my heart, and the lightness of 69kg of useful things that would accompany us across the globe. Even better was my new status: time millionaire – time traveller! Plus, my family was really excited, and Vera and I had rarely laughed as much as we had in recent weeks. In addition, I could look myself in the eye without scaring myself.

I still felt nervous, though. What if the whole thing was even half as unrealistic as our relatives and friends had forecast? What would happen if, after eight weeks, we realised that we weren't having fun? Or, to be more precise – how could we know which bits would be fun? We hadn't made any more concrete plans for our trip. There were no to-do lists for the million minutes ahead.

So: what were those 'really nice things' Nina had asked for – the things for which we were about to abandon pretty much everything?

# IN SEARCH OF THE REALLY NICE THINGS

THE SMALL ISLAND OF PHRA THONG IS ONLY A FEW nautical kilometres off the coast of Thailand, not far from the border with Myanmar, and has evidently been bought up wholesale by a handful of wealthy individuals and luxury resort companies. If you're an A-list VIP, you presumably hear about these resorts from another A-list VIP. If you're a B- or C-list VIP, or even an ordinary individual, your wanderings around the island will sooner or later bring you up against some well-guarded fences. Peer through these fences and you will see magnificent gardens with armies of staff scurrying about among frangipanis and bougainvilleas and hibiscuses. Prices are available on demand, and only if they take you seriously. A single night in a villa in one of these deluxe establishments starts at several hundred dollars (they're exclusive, which goes without saying). Where it ends is anybody's guess. Different customers have different needs.

It seemed that ordinary tourism was practically non-existent here. The hand-picked guests had entire beaches to themselves, like shipwrecked sailors – except that there were liveried waiters going back and forth between them, collecting cocktail requests and seafood orders for the five-course 'grand dinner'. All this, of course, rather overstretched our budget. But because we'd decided to reward ourselves for the strenuous months of travel preparations in Bonn by doing nothing at all for a while, and because Vera could drive an even harder bargain than the resort managers, we had somehow wangled a last-minute deal in the most modest house in the cheapest resort. Our new residence was called Baan Mak, a three-storey building made entirely of tropical timber – there was even a tree incorporated, Hundertwasser-style, in the architecture. The management blurb explained that the eco-resort had been especially constructed to make you feel 'part of the forest'. To Nina's delight, larger-than-life insects were an inherent feature of the 'forest experience', but there were beautiful mosquito nets hanging over the beds like baldachins, and if you stayed right in the middle of the bed and pulled up your feet, you were barely bitten. Many visitors to the island seemed to regard our resort as third-class accommodation, just about good enough for their accompanying staff – hairdressers, pedicurists and bodyguards. We disagreed: for us it was a just-affordable dose of doing nothing.

And things were to get even better. Every now and then, some coked-up fund manager somewhere in the United States screws up big time and one of those investment funds with equity, wealth or fidelity in its name loses almost three-quarters of its value within days. No one understands, of course, where all the money can have gone; it vanishes as mysteriously as it appeared. There is a flurry of crisis meetings and press conferences; troops of expensive lawyers scan the globe for people who might have cause for anger – and lo and behold, a great many people are indeed fighting for the last scraps of their once-proud risk capital, like the grey gentlemen in Michael Ende's fantasy novel *Momo* fighting for their time cigars.

Some bays away from Baan Mak there were two very nice American women staying in a villa – very nice, but not very relaxed. Even on this incredible island, they kept up their habit of checking the stock market every hour. They were extremely fond of children but in a rather clumsy way, like people who love animals but don't know how to handle them. Once, one of them, Catherine, picked up Mr Simon by taking hold of one of his arms and pulling him into the air. When he began to protest at this irregular treatment, she simply dropped the dangling baby back onto the sand (he managed to keep his arm). Catherine couldn't get enough of Mr Simon – what an *incredibly* gorgeous baby, what an *adorable* smile, and so on. And then one day, just as Nina and I almost had them playing ball with us, Catherine and her friend noticed that their pet investment fund had taken a tumble, and off they went in a cloud of dust. At any rate, they were in enough of a hurry to bribe their way onto a fully booked flight home. A lightning move like that takes some doing in Thailand, with all those Buddhists working at the airport.

Of course, you can't cancel a booking on an exclusive premium villa. Or maybe that kind of thing just isn't done in the top-price segment. Who knows? The fact is, we found ourselves moving out of Baan Mak and accepting ten days in the Americans' stunning villa – inclusive, it goes without saying – as the two women boarded a speedboat with three 75hp engines (that's equivalent to more than 200 horses in harness) and vanished over the horizon, waving.

*    *    *

It was only a fortnight earlier that we had pulled our lumbering suitcases over the cold, wet streets of Bonn, the winter moon reflected in the puddles on the dark grey cobblestones. And now here we were in the dazzling light of the tropical sun, on the private beachfront deck of the most luxurious house I had ever set foot in. We called it the veranda, but this outside construction was so large that even when all four of us were on it together, we felt lost. It was also built so close to the water that the glassy waves vanished somewhere underneath it whenever the tide was in. If anything fell into the water, that was the end of it. With a baby in tow, this was inconvenient, to say the least. Then there were the coconut palms sticking up out of the veranda – how were we supposed to play ball, with them in the way? The house itself was crammed with Asian antiques, including a collection of fat Buddhas with XXL earlobes, which Nina immediately fell in love with, and a lot of tasteful modern art installations. Our nearest neighbour lived out of sight some 200 metres down the beach – 'to guarantee exclusive privacy', the manager politely explained to us. I wondered whether he was alluding to Mr Simon's night-time yelling, but he was too professional to let his thoughts show. It was at about this time that I had begun to ask myself whether Mr Simon could be described as a *screamer*, but it's no good overreacting when you're a parent.

I'd always thought of a house on the water as the epitome of romanticism, but I soon realised that you have to have reached an advanced stage of Zen to appreciate the charm of it. At every big wave I heard in the dark, I would think, *this is it – this time the water's coming into the house* – and I spent the best part of the first three nights jumping out of bed and groping about on the wooden floorboards to feel if they were wet. They weren't. Once I was attacked by a gecko which, in the dim light of dawn, mistook my finger for goodness knows what. That didn't do anything to improve my sleep. It's amazing, the way we'll find something to moan about, even in the lap of luxury. Vera bore everything with fortitude, for which I was grateful. She was nice enough to point out that we were 'only just starting out' and 'probably all still a bit dazed'. Besides, we could catch up on sleep in the afternoon. All it took was one of those giant hammocks that came with the house and a Mr Simon exhausted from his morning's circumnavigation of the beach.

If you took the narrow sandy path that wound through the resort's private forest, and wandered along among the hundreds of hermit crabs that dragged their shells through the sand, day in, day out, as uncomplaining as Sisyphus, you eventually came to the narrowest point of the island. Here you had to make a choice. The left fork led to the Indian Ocean. Set sail from there, out onto the open sea, and you would, with a bit of luck, see the coast of East India appear on the horizon a few weeks later. The right fork, meanwhile, led to a huge shallow-water lagoon surrounded by palm-covered rocky islands. A perfect setting for a film. In fact, wherever you went here, you felt as if you'd landed in one of those movies where a sozzled digital-effects crew has gone in for some heavy-handed backdrop enhancement. Past the lagoon and around a small promontory was a bay where even Robinson Crusoe would have felt lonely. What an incredible beginning to a journey. It can't, I thought, get better than this.

*   *   *

We were barely two weeks into our journey and we were already on a tropical island. And we had time. What Vera and I hadn't yet worked out was what to do with it. What did Adam and Eve get up to all day before they were thrown out of Paradise (apart from the obvious)?

This journey was different from any I had undertaken before; I had no idea how it would end. That made it hard to make plans. At home in Bonn, I had only rarely wondered how best we would use the seeming eternity of those million minutes. My Massive Adult Imagination Deficit led to ideas that fell into the category *useful and meaningful* – the kinds of activities that would *get me somewhere*, like learning a new language or doing a correspondence course. Should be doable, I thought – and then at some point I would have to get round to rethinking my career options. 'You like to have a project, don't you?' Vera remarked when I shared my ideas. But strangely, from the moment we'd jumped out of the boat onto the shore of this island, I'd forgotten all about those useful projects.

Unlike me, Nina didn't have the slightest difficulty in filling a million minutes. I expect that all children the world over know almost instinctively what the *really nice things* are. They're naturals at it. Picasso allegedly said that it took him all his life to recover the naivety of his childhood. Here on this remote island, I began to understand what he meant.

To my surprise, we all turned out to want pretty much the same thing. It wasn't that we'd talked about it at any length; it just *happened*. And we got up to some fairly strange things. I didn't really notice at the time, and there was no one to make sarcastic remarks, but when I looked back through my journal after the first weeks on

Ko Phra Thong, it suddenly hit me. I had written: *most of the very nice things are moments.* But the most frequent entries consisted of a string of unconnected words and phrases: *mussel field on north beach (long square mussels with mother-of-pearl shells!), bonfire again,* or: *coconut catastrophe (borrow machete?), excursion (rocky bay in west: sea urchins!).* The word *sandcastle* featured three times. It was kids' stuff! I imagined my boss in Bonn asking me in his usual undertone at the weekly research group meeting: 'So what are you up to at the moment?' That was always his cue for us to report on the progress we were making on our projects. I saw myself in front of all my colleagues and former students, reading aloud from my journal: *square mussels, coconut catastrophe…*

But that's the way humans are. Throw them out of a tour bus anywhere high enough for a decent view and they'll start building cairns. Set them around a fire and they'll stare into the embers as if hypnotised. Put some music on and they'll start making jerky, unflattering movements. Place a ball on the ground in front of a group of humans and we all know what will happen, the world over. People spend hours waiting for the big wave, or try, against their better knowledge, to hold back an entire ocean with a sandcastle. They don't give up easily. They bury their arms and legs – and those of others – in the sand. They sit underwater; they pretend that stars are organised into patterns; they wait for shooting stars at night and pink clouds in the evening. They make snowballs and throw them at people they like. All these activities come easier if there happen to be a few children around, when it's just a question of joining in. (In the absence of children, you can consume neurotoxic substances, or call your games 'sport' and pay to watch them.) You might say you've had a *flow experience* à la Csikszentmihalyi, the psychologist who invented the concept, or that you've been *in the zone* – some people call it mindfulness – and everyone will know what you're talking about. All this kids' stuff must be inherent to our nature, deeply ingrained in us. Why did it mean so much to me when I finally found a red double-twisted shell after crawling around on the beach for an hour? It felt as if something inside me was stirring into life after years of lying dormant.

*   *   *

There was only one item on the programme that day: the lonely bay. Nina had already rounded the corner, but Vera and I still had to gather up the beach toys – and Mr Simon, who was on a mission to consume as much sand as possible. The first mouthful didn't bother us too much; there's no accounting for taste, but we were counting on the high salt content putting him off. Mr Simon, however, seemed to find it delectable, and since his main mode of movement was to slither along on his tummy, all he had to do was open his mouth, thrust down his head and push himself forward, caterpillar-like, with his knees. The overall effect was that of a whale gliding through a cloud of plankton. For a while we stood and stared at him, determined to remain faithful to our parenting principles – let children learn from their mistakes – but after about a kilo of sand, we decided that our principles were best abandoned.

As I turned the corner with the bags full of buckets and spades, I saw Nina, already settled on the sand. She waved me over and pointed at the beach with a look of appreciation.

'They're very funny here,' she whispered.

The men on our island were tall, rarely much under six foot. They were not particularly shy, dyed their skin in shades ranging from salmon to lobster and favoured pastel-coloured Calvin Klein shorts. Once a year, before the *big rain that doesn't stop*, the males seem to gather in this secret bay on the island of Phra Thong to celebrate the old ceremonies and tribal rituals.

Nina was right: about 20 men had worked themselves collectively into a very strange state on the beach before us. Perhaps the correct word to describe them was Nina's *enthusiasmed*. Some of them were bellowing like rutting stags, although there wasn't a female in sight. Others were bouncing apparently aimlessly along the beach, emitting sharp cries. Others again seemed to favour a more gregarious approach and were roaring in unison, even though they were standing right next to each other. I think Nina imagined that here on this beach, far from screwed-up Western civilisation, we had stumbled upon indigenous people of the Indian Ocean involved in a kind of initiation rite. Given what the men were doing, this was completely plausible. She was thrilled. At last she had found a country where people knew how to behave – how to make something of their lives.

'Qui-et,' she whispered insistently, looking at me with raised eyebrows. She had a point: perhaps it was wisest not to disturb them.

The challenge of the day was clear enough. The men, participants in an exclusive leadership seminar organised by a global coaching agency for successful top managers who wanted to be even more successful, had been asked to construct rafts out of a variety of components – polystyrene blocks, brightly coloured plastic buoys, thick ropes, wooden poles and anything else they happened to find on the beach. Once the rafts were complete, each team had to send out an emissary to paddle around a buoy about 30 metres from the shore and return to the beach, noisily cheered on by his teammates. (The team-building nature of the challenge meant that shouting was mandatory.) The winning team was the one whose emissary set foot ashore first and tore a red stake from the ground with a dramatic flourish – fundamentally altered, of course, by this life-changing exercise.

The whole thing was carried out feverishly, not to say hysterically. While some men rushed off to the coconut palms on the shore and returned laden with palm fronds and driftwood (to roars of appreciation), others proudly presented armfuls of coconuts to their teammates (to louder roars). You had to be careful: only the old, pale brown coconuts made suitable floats; the green ones pulled you under (Nina and I had experimented already). A third group, meanwhile, were tugging at ropes like men possessed in order to lash the buoys fast to the sticks. These ones had to roar for themselves, because the others were busy. In the middle of this mayhem stood an imposing figure – a phenotype foreign legionary – not big, but with an aura of dominance and glacial eyes. He could roar louder than any of them and did so, issuing a mixture of orders, curses and insults, like a commander addressing a bunch of galley slaves. He clearly had oodles of leadership qualities. I thought I caught words like *wusses*, *wimps* and other similarly motivating names. I suppose that being the coach, he had to give the men their money's worth. No wonder the atmosphere was hotting up by the time the first two groups dragged their rafts towards the waves.

'They're playing,' Nina said to me, staring raptly at the men, her voice almost admiring.

At such times I often found myself wondering whether our father – daughter relationship wasn't a front for an experiment, with me as the test subject. The pedagogical subtext of our conversations cropped up too often for me to be just imagining it. Nina evidently wanted me to learn a thing or two from these men, and she expected me to work that out for myself. Sometimes, being 'parented' by a five-year-old could be quite a challenge.

'Look as if we're playing games, don't we?' a voice panted at my side, in a refined English accent.

I jumped; I hadn't seen the man coming. He'd been gathering palm fronds down by the shore and was covered in scratches, and had large sunburn blisters on his shoulders and sweat pouring down his nose. I assumed an innocent expression and hurriedly said no, not at all, then glanced at Nina, who was clearly wondering how best to congratulate this noble native. Luckily her English wasn't good enough for her to say anything compromising. The man explained that *all this* – he swept his arm over the beach – was part of a prestigious seminar programme developed in association with leading psychologists and CEOs. I nodded, impressed, pleased that the games I came up with for the children so closely resembled cutting-edge research. He said his name was Damian, and maybe we'd see each other in the bar some evening. Before I could introduce us, he'd corrected himself. 'Well, George, actually, George Damian. Terribly sorry, but I have to go now.' And off he went with his palm fronds.

As it happened, George and I missed each other in the bar, and the next time I saw him he was at the dock in a high-powered speedboat bound for the mainland. It made a curious picture, he and the other managers huddled in Day-Glo yellow lifejackets, staring at the water, suddenly subdued. Game over, I thought, and wondered how they'd feel when they went back to the office in a couple of days. For a second it occurred to me that I, too… but I dismissed that thought. It was one I could put on hold for some time.

'What are they doing today?' Nina asked. I was leaning against the dock's wooden fence and Nina, as always, was leaning against me to steady herself. The jetty was on the wobbly side.

'Hmm, I guess they've finished playing.' And so that it didn't sound too sad, I added, 'They're going home now.'

'Oh,' said Nina. She looked disappointed. 'They were very good at playing, those men.'

In my journal I had started a section called *Aspects of Paradise*. All I'd written so far was: *maybe paradise is actually childhood?*

\* \* \*

That evening we sat on the beach by a bonfire, watching the sparks sally forth into the night sky. The sun had said goodbye by way of what the local people called *a supernatural sunset*. Nina was already out for the count on the sand. She always fought sleep for as long as she could, determined not to waste a second of the day, but as the evening wore on, she would grow slower and slower, eventually stopping mid-movement, the way a clock stops when it needs to be wound. One hand was resting on a coconut, presumably a special nut that mustn't be lost, even if there were ten thousand others lying on the beach. Her other hand clutched a stick. Children can sleep anywhere. Mr Simon lay snuggled up on Vera's lap.

Beany, the foreign legionary, and some of his colleagues had stayed on for a kind of debriefing. We'd talked a bit over the last few days, and that evening they'd invited us to a private beach barbecue. It turned out that Beany had ridden a rollercoaster career from proud school dropout and kite-surfing pro to sport psychologist and World Cup coach, eventually becoming what he called a *reason-seller*. I hadn't been able to resist pestering him about the managers' seminar, privately wondering if it might hold a future job for me. I had a decent repertoire of English swear words, and was sure that with Nina as my creative director, I could develop some successful leadership and team-building tools. I already had a new section in my journal entitled *Potential Jobs*. First on the list was *organising corporate manager games on islands*.

'Actually,' Beany said, 'the main focus isn't on management skills. What we do is sell reasons. When you've made it in your career as far as these lads have, you need a bloody good excuse to invest your precious time in building a raft or staring into a fire.'

We stared into the fire.

'Sure, we have plenty of know-how on board – communication and leadership techniques, change management, the whole gamut. We're totally professional. But the deal is this: the resort keeps your average tourist at bay. Then we can pretend and they can pretend they're only pretending to amuse themselves. The more expensive it is, the more authentic it becomes. But just for a few days, we put things they really want on their agenda: shouting, playing, fun fights, acting as kings and slaves, all kinds of survival games – building sandcastles, for all I care – the things they really want to do, you see? Preferably without suncream so that they really *feel*.' Beany smiled. 'Basically, they pay us lots of money for us to give them a halfway official reason to enjoy the things that children love to do.'

He looked at the fire again, a satisfied smile on his face. And I thought to myself how surprised he'd be if he knew how well I understood. Then I looked across at my three best reasons, cuddled up next to the fire, and considered that I'd done pretty well so far.

# SAME SAME BUT DIFFERENT

60,000TH MINUTE
KO YAO YAI
YAO ARCHIPELAGO (7°58'N, 98°35'E)
PHANG NGA BAY, THAILAND

**culture shock**, *n*. The emotions and impressions experienced by a person suddenly brought into contact with an unfamiliar culture. Often this is subdivided into several phases, for example an initial phase of euphoria (*honeymoon*), followed by a sudden shocked sense of being out of place (*crisis*)…

OUR STAY ON KO PHRA THONG COULD HARDLY HAVE been more euphoric or honeymoon-like. But when our days of pampered relaxation in the luxury beachfront villa came to an end, we moved on with a light heart, lured by the thought of adventures in a new and unfamiliar world. I was curious to see what reactions it would provoke in Nina, whose imagination was already exuberant.

We began by spending a fortnight or so sightseeing on the Thai mainland, and ended up on the island of Yao Yai nearly six weeks into our trip – a sleepy place, considering that two hours away by boat, in Phuket, the package tourists start quarrelling over the sun loungers at dawn. Unlike the high-end resort world of Ko Phra Thong, Ko Yao Yai is a genuine Thai island with its own people, habits and customs. It isn't big; you can get from the southern end to the northernmost tip in half an hour on a moped. The one main road, which branches off into dirt tracks here and there, takes you past a handful of idyllic fishing villages; between these villages, small resorts are scattered along the coast, hugging the bays. There are no official sights to see and rural life goes on, largely untouched by tourism. The biggest supermarkets are about the size of a large sitting room, and though 75% of the shelves are stocked with packets of crisps and products bearing the ubiquitous Coca-Cola logo, there are also strips of salt fish, buckets of chopped squid, unfamiliar-smelling meat hanging from hooks on the ceiling and crates of exotic fruit. The yellow fist-sized mangos were among the most delicious things I have ever eaten.

The boatman who took us on board at Phuket's Ranong Pier couldn't speak highly enough of his native island. For one thing, the people of Ko Yao Yai were predominantly Muslim. 'You know Muslims? Muslims are good people!' He told us it was 'very quiet' on the island. 'No party,' he added, with a glance at Nina and Mr Simon. When I tested this with a look of sad disappointment, he hurried to qualify the statement. 'OK, some party, of course. Big party, you know.'

Tourism probably accounted for a substantial part of the island's revenue, so if there was a demand for it, the locals would organise a lavish party to entertain any visitors who were at a loose end. Other than that, they earned a livelihood from growing rubber. It takes about a thousand rubber trees to generate enough income to feed one islander, so it's hardly surprising that the island's rainforests have given way to rubber plantations: tens of thousands of perfectly straight trees in long rows, like forests of pillars. The children on the island don't inherit houses, which rarely hold out against the climate and the termites for more than 30 years; they inherit the trees planted for them by their parents instead.

Wherever we went, we were welcomed with great warmth and even greater curiosity; another sign that tourists were relatively rare here.

When we arrived, children at the roadside pointed and giggled at us as we tripped over the chickens under our feet. Eventually, the boldest of them approached us and, after some hesitation, reached out to touch Nina's light blonde hair. The results of this experiment were discussed extensively, with much excited chattering; they then fell to giggling again. Mr Simon was also quite an attraction. Blond and blue-eyed and still quite pale-skinned thanks to the factor 50 sunscreen, he was forever being patted and pawed. If you're planning to travel in this part of the world with a baby and wish to avoid coming to blows over the poor little thing, you should know that it is perfectly normal here for people to tear your child out of your arms without warning and disappear with it, wreathed in smiles. We had no need to sign up for some expensive kids' club; it was enough to go out to eat. Within minutes, some lovely female employee would descend on Mr Simon and tell us he had *eyes beautiful smile yes*. He was generally thrilled to be kidnapped. Sometimes he'd be gone a full quarter of an hour, but he almost always came back looking very pleased with himself. Only the cooks complained that he didn't eat enough. He wasn't *nice fat*. If they'd had their way, they'd have taken over for a few months until Mr Simon had bulked up a bit.

We had taken the simplest guest house we could find, for the monthly rent of our flat in Bonn, we could afford to stay here for many months, if we wanted to. This place was totally different from the accommodation we had enjoyed on Ko Phra Thong, but once we were used to the cold water, sleeping on beds made from pallets, patched-up mosquito nets, threadbare towels and the clattering of a prehistoric overhead fan all night, it was a fine adventure.

'Do you miss the posh villa on Ko Phra Thong?' I asked Nina one morning.

She thought for a moment. 'I miss the Buddhas on the shelves, but I love the snugness of sleeping all together in one room again,' she said.

That summed up the benefits.

\* \* \*

There was no ignoring that this was a foreign culture. The very first morning, I was woken by Nina frantically shaking my shoulder.

'Daddy, someone's shouting out there!' she whispered excitedly, her finger jabbing the darkness.

I listened and soon realised what it was. About 100 metres from our little bed and breakfast was a minaret. Somebody clearly took his job seriously and had a powerful megaphone to help him. We were later told that Mr Islam was the best singer on the island and performed his duty with the passion of a Caruso.

'That's a muezzin. They sing to remind the people here to pray in the mornings. Like church bells in Germany.'

'Do we have to pray too?'

'No, we're not Muslim.' I pulled her over to me. 'Come here, it's still time to sleep.'

For a moment, Nina listened to the singing with its unfamiliar intervals. Then, in rather pitying tones, she said, 'He can't sing.'

'No, he sings *differently* from us, that's all. The people here like different songs. They would probably think "Frère Jacques" sounded all wrong.'

'But "Frère Jacques" is lovely.'

I decided not to pursue the topic, and it was too early in the morning for complicated explanations. Let the Muslim brethren go about their duties. I pulled Nina under the duvet to me without another word, and we were soon asleep again.

For breakfast there was muesli with yoghurt and bananas.

'Like at home,' Nina observed with satisfaction. Then something made a funny noise in her mouth. 'It's got stones in,' she said in disgust.

Seedless bananas are for spoilt Western Europeans. Thai bananas have up to 12 pea-sized seeds per fruit.

'I can't believe it,' Nina said, staring at the black seed in her hand.

'Well, it would appear to be there, whether you believe it or not,' I replied rather pretentiously, glad of this uncontroversial example of intercultural difference. 'The further from home you travel, the more things you discover.'

Nina was arranging the banana seeds into patterns on the table.

After a few minutes, she said: 'We're a long way from home here, aren't we?'

'A very long way,' I said. 'About a month and a half – or 9,000 kilometres.'

She concentrated on seeding bananas, making a thorough two-handed job of it. Then: 'Do they have flying dogs here?'

I should have known that was coming. 'No, of course not. Dogs can't fly.'

'But when we were at home in Bonn you asked Mum if she knew that some dogs can fly,' she said.

'OK, but I didn't really mean it. Dogs can't fly.'

'How do you know?' Nina was nothing if not stubborn.

Once again I was up to my neck in an epistemological quagmire. I recalled a seminar about the philosopher Karl Popper in my second year at university. What we call reality is, in fact, only the part of reality that we know. Until explorers in Australia discovered black swans, all swans were white. Black swans didn't exist – never mind that they'd been paddling around the inlets of western Australia for tens of thousands of years.

I didn't want to get onto thin ice. 'If ever we see such a thing as a flying dog, then flying dogs exist, all right?'

Nina gave me a funny look, but seemed satisfied for the time being.

A few days later we decided to hire a moped. We were given a warm welcome by the owner of the scooter rental shop, who also ran the filling station, fixed cars, kept an Internet cafe and, of course, sold crisps. No, he didn't have two mopeds for hire, but the big one over there in the corner might have been made for us. Vera looked doubtfully at me. By European standards there was no way the vehicle was designed to accommodate four people. The man had seen the glance and wasted no time.

'We are Thailand, you know? Here no problem in Thailand. You know,' he declared, 'is good for you people and five people and six people.'

He dusted the saddle. We debated the matter for a while until Vera eventually laughed and gave in. That was the usual pattern. Since Mr Simon was not yet qualified to give an opinion, Nina and I were in a comfortable two-thirds majority with our often rather radical suggestions. It was Nina and I who had introduced the democratic family vote and it worked a treat. A moped made for four; why not? After all, the journey was the goal. Delighted by our grassroots democracy, the man handed it over, making a point of telling us that the brake worked. Then he skilfully sucked petrol into the hose until it ran into the tank all by itself. Nina threw me a look of astonishment, but said nothing.

Balanced on the moped with a rucksack full of yellow mangos – yet another line of business pursued by our enterprising moped owner – we set off for Lo Paret beach, a place we'd already visited a few times on foot. Between an old sagging concrete pier and a small wood, fishermen's children ran about as they waited for their fathers to return with their catch. It was touching to see them play with the crabs on the beach. Sometimes they even took them for walks on leads, like the old ladies who walked their little dogs by the Rhine in Bonn. Same same…

Nina was thrilled. An exotic pet? She wasn't going to let a chance like that pass her by. She had a special relationship with animals as it was, which was maybe something to do with her huge capacity for patience. She approached animals with such calm that even the most psychotic cat would end up rubbing itself against her legs, purring. It was like horse whispering. When Nina dipped a hand into the quarry ponds we sometimes drove to from Bonn, she only had to move her fingers in a certain way and the frogs came swimming over. Once, in the south of France, I even saw her stand up to her waist in a pretty cold lake, motionless for over an hour and a half, until the wild perch came so close she was able to stroke their backs. The fisherman next to us, who'd been trying to catch a fish for two days, packed up and left, grumbling to himself.

Now Nina began careful, strategic work on Project Pet Acquisition. She started by constructing a replica of our luxury villa, a coconut home with a beachfront deck, a saltwater pool and a bordering plantation of a thousand bathmat trees to attract her quarry. Her idea of living standards had evidently been upgraded by her travels. But there was also a shed *stocked up for the winter* (Nina still had one foot in the old world). Of course, we'd only been in the tropics for just under two months, and for all she knew, they might have European seasons here. Finally, everything was ready for the crabs to move into their new abode.

But the crabs on Ko Yao Yai begged to differ – and who can blame them? If they didn't manage to scuttle under a rock or into the sea in time, they'd open their formidable shiny crimson pincers and stretch them out towards anyone who came too close. They also blew a lot of bubbles and frothed away to themselves, making curious crunching sounds, presumably a sign of annoyance or warning – not that we needed any reminding that some of them had pincers thicker than my fingers. Nina decided that patience was the way forward. She spent hours wriggling commando-style over the sand in slow motion, in one hand a collar with a special loop, in the other a variety of foodstuffs. Breakfast was originally to be *delicious special sliced bread*, but when that was rejected, she tried pieces of coconut with fresh leaves. Next came little bits of fish, and eventually she resorted to bananas. Specially deseeded. *So they don't choke.* All to no avail.

Nina coaxed the crabs with honeyed words. 'You'll soon see how good it tastes! I have a house for you, too.' One specimen was even told, 'If you're good, you can come to Australia with me.'

But despite such prospects, the crabs seemed unable to muster much enthusiasm. A three-foot-something blonde girl in glasses chattering away at them non-stop wasn't part of their entertainment routine. How else to explain why the fishermen's children got on so much better with the little beasts than Nina? A different species of crab? The right kind of food? Voodoo?

After another whole hour of futile attempts to woo the crabs, Nina came back to us.

'This has never happened to me,' she said, shaking her head dejectedly. 'I've explained everything to them.'

I tried to make it easier for her. I wanted to tell her that crabs don't like people, but the fishermen's children at the other end of the bay were evidence to the contrary. 'Maybe they don't understand you.'

Nina screwed up her nose and thought for a long time.

Then she said, 'How do you say *don't be scared* in Thailandish?'

After landing their long-tail boats in the next bay, the fishermen would spend the rest of the day cleaning and gutting the fish and patching their nets. One of them sometimes wandered past our beach. He'd passed us the day before, but without taking any notice of Nina; a fisherman is a busy man. This time, though, he stopped, and for a while stood and watched Nina and her attempts at crab-catching. Then he walked over to her, squatted down and began to talk to her in his language in a friendly way, gesticulating. Nina replied in German, telling him her dilemma. Did he have an explanation? They went on like this for some time, unable to understand a word of each other's languages, but apparently managing to amuse themselves because I kept hearing them laugh.

Eventually the fisherman got up and stalked purposefully among the rocks. Then suddenly, he plunged a hand into a rockpool and pulled out a crab. First try, first hit! It had taken him under ten seconds. It was his job, of course, and I guessed he'd been catching fish ever since he could walk. He adroitly held the flailing crustacean in such a way that its extended pincers couldn't reach his wrist, and swung it back and forth in front of Nina, a fine specimen, its shimmering colours shifting between dark blue and pale pink, its round black eyes on telescopic stalks swivelling in all directions. You could tell that Nina was pleased that her efforts were finally at an end: everything else would sort itself out once the crab saw what a magnificent residence she had designed for it.

I went over to the two of them.

'He's so nice,' she said to me, pointing at the fisherman. Then she held out her collar to him.

The fisherman gave a friendly nod and then ripped the first pincer off the crab, which made a very ugly noise indeed. The pincer landed right at Nina's feet. She just had time to look up again before the fisherman grabbed the second pincer. This one didn't come away directly at the shell, but at one of the leg joints; something soft and white came away with it and hung limply from the crab. The fisherman skilfully looped the collar around the body and, with a big smile on his face, held out the twitching creature to Nina, in both hands, because that is a sign of politeness in Thailand. He said something that was presumably the Thai equivalent of *et voilà*.

Nina was stiff with shock, gasping for breath, eyes wide. She stared at the man aghast; her hands – only a second ago held out to him expectantly – jerked back.

'What have you done? You've…' She turned to me, switching addressee mid-sentence. 'He's ripped out the crab's arms.'

The three of us stared at the pincers dancing on the ground between her feet. A thick, dark blue liquid was running out of one of them. The crab, meanwhile, was furiously blowing bubbles; they were even frothing up out of its stumps. It was gruesome, even for me, and I've seen my fair share of anti-meat videos.

Profound sobbing from below right. 'They'll never go back on again.'

Too right they wouldn't. It seemed that the crabs being lovingly taken for walks by the local children had actually been zombies. Throwaway pets.

The fisherman's hands, holding the horror crab, had dropped slightly. For a moment he stared at Nina through narrowed eyes. Perhaps he was thinking to himself that these Western children were rude, ungrateful so-and-sos, not to mention ridiculously sentimental. What use was a child like that at half past three in the morning in stormy seas and high waves, or when the trawl net was caught in the corals again? What good was an oversensitive child when a fish had bitten someone's hand or a drift line had cut deep into someone's arm?

He took a step towards the sea and nudged one of the still-twitching pincers into the water with his foot. Then he turned a questioning eye on Nina. It looked like an offer of reconciliation. Another nudge. Now the second pincer was rolled back and forth over the sand by the little waves. But of course, Nina was not to be consoled by local fish-waste disposal methods. She was beside herself, alternately sobbing and yelling at the fisherman with every one of her six swear words. I was glad he couldn't understand what she was saying, and resolved to remind her that some expressions are best reserved for private use. But anger can be understood across cultures and the fisherman could see that Nina wasn't happy. He thought there must be something the matter with her – and she thought there must be something the matter with him.

He turned and set off back to his own family with a shrug, the crab flailing in his hand. At least he took the thing with him.

*   *   *

The second phase of culture shock, *crisis*, is said to be marked by 'surprise and outrage at discovering the extent of cultural difference'. Two months into our journey, the crisis had hit us. On the beach we held a family council to which Mr Simon contributed with loud snores. Our topic: *the nastiest man in the world.*

'He didn't mean to be horrid,' I said.

'Yes, he did. He laughed.' Nina had clenched her hands into fists and was shaking her head – always a sign of maximum protest. It seemed that the *horrid man*'s worst crime was pretending to be nice while he did the ghastly deed.

'He wanted to help you. He wanted to give you a crab.'

'But you said' – defiantly – 'that you must never hurt animals.'

It occurred to me then that apart from Vera, everyone in the family loved eating meat. Nina adored prawns in garlic sauce; but it would probably be wise to avoid the vegetarian debate just now.

'That's at home in Germany. The fishermen here have different rules. Maybe there are other things they're not allowed to do that are perfectly fine for us.'

Tolerance of other cultures seemed to be a tricky topic, for parents *and* children. Hadn't I explained a hundred times that there were clear rules that we stuck to because they were sensible (changing into our swimming costumes *before* going in the water, for instance)? That it was best to stick to these rules *all the time* (yes, you're going to clean your teeth tonight, just like every other night). And that they applied to *everyone* (no, Simon really isn't allowed to stay up later than you). So much for the theory. How was a kid supposed to understand when someone not only broke the rules, but broke them with a big smile on his face?

'This is all terrible,' Nina raged.

There was no consoling her; the shock was still too deep. She was clearly going to need a little time before she was ready for the third phase of culture shock: *recovery.* But after a few strangely quiet days – you could see the little cogs whirring – her mood began to improve, though she did make a point of avoiding the fishermen and the crabs, preferring to stick to the lower-maintenance hermit crabs in their shell houses.

After our crisis meeting, Vera and I had almost expected her to utter the dreaded words, 'I want to go home,' or, 'How long is this holiday going on for?' We had resolved to take such warning signals seriously and, if necessary, rethink our plans. But the words never came. However sorry I was about the crab episode, I was thrilled by the implications. After all, one goal of our travels was to take us beyond our own horizons. In my journal I wrote: *Should distance of travel really be measured in kilometres? New unit of measurement: adventure. Surprises, culture shock? Trouble reintegrating afterwards?*

Of course, I wasn't sure how small children deal with such experiences. But Nina wouldn't have been Nina if she hadn't found her own way of coming to terms with the episode and turning it to her own use. The last phase of culture shock, *adaptation*, is said to have been reached when 'the affected person begins to adopt behavioural traits from the foreign culture'.

One evening, we got back to the bed and breakfast at dusk. We were exhausted from a long boat tour around the islands of Phang Nga Bay, famous for its limestone cliffs, but instead of going straight to bed as I'd asked her, Nina escaped into the corridor. This was nothing unusual – but this time, the situation took an unexpected turn.

'Come on, off to bed now!'

No reaction; she simply went on playing.

'I told you to get ready for bed.'

At this point, most children take one of three possible tacks, familiar to all parents in all universes: the *are-you-really-going-to-be-that-horrible* approach, the negotiation marathon or the slow-motion huff.

But we didn't get any of those; only demonstrative silence.

I went on with my routine monologue. 'Eight o'clock is bedtime.'

At last Nina looked up. She stared at me in feigned astonishment. 'You mean, like in Germany? But we're in Thailand now.'

I laughed and gave in. I felt she'd earned an extra hour of 'Thai time'.

The next morning, she bested me again. In a boat on our way to the tiny island of Khai Nok, we ran into a school of flying fish. They seemed to have decided to leap right over our boat, and we ducked for cover as the first fish flew, because getting one in your face is not the most agreeable of sensations. Only Nina remained sitting up.

'I knew it!' she cried, waving her arms wildly through the air. 'I knew it. They're fish, but they can fly!'

Our eyes met. I could see it wasn't always going to be easy travelling with her through the parallel universes of our million minutes, but it was going to be great.

# STONE LETTUCE

THE FOUR SKY-HIGH TOWERS OF THE PRINCE PALACE
Hotel in central Bangkok are stuffed so full of luxury that it's little
short of a miracle they don't collapse under their own weight. The
place is dripping with dark tropical-wood panelling, yards of brass,
huge mirrors, thick slabs of marble, fans, peacock feathers, vases of
imported cherry blossom and Asian sculptures in red jasper, giltwood
or jade. But the pièce de résistance of this collection of curiosities is
on the 12th floor of Tower Two: displayed on a special plinth in the
middle of a hall, like Napoleon's tomb in the Invalides, and bathed
in the golden glow of its own spotlights, lies a heavy object in green
jade, about a metre and a half long and at least half a metre high. If
you venture nearer – in spite of the sign instructing you not to – you
will see that this monumental object is a vast semi-precious Chinese
leaf. Apparently, the Chinese word for cabbage sounds exactly like the
word for money, and because of this linguistic accident, cabbages are
a symbol of wealth. There are even statues of the Buddha holding a
cabbage in his hand – somewhat incongruously, as the Buddha isn't
someone I associate with worldly wealth. But here, in the Prince
Palace, the message is unequivocal. The hotel stands on the site of the
former palace of Prince Krom Luang Nakhon Chaisri Suradej, son of
the great Rama V, a powerful king of Siam.

\* \* \*

Our triumphal entry into the Prince Palace caused something of a stir. The three liveried porters stared in disbelief as we climbed out of the taxi and made for the hotel lobby. The tallest of them gave the taxi driver a disapproving look, but he shrugged it off; he had, after all, twice asked us whether we were sure about the address – a third time and he'd have risked losing his tip. One of the other porters gave us as professional a greeting as he could muster and, amid Nina's vociferous attempts to defend our belongings, tried to heave one of our rucksacks onto a brass-studded luggage trolley. The last porter ran up to reception, taking the stairs two at a time – presumably to warn his boss.

None of us had had a haircut since leaving Bonn three months before, and we hadn't bothered much with brushes and combs either. Nina and Mr Simon, in particular, were shaggy-headed from the daily assault of sun, sunscreen and saltwater: their hair stuck up every which way. Nina's glasses, held together with plasters in four places, were reluctant to stay on her nose. (Her spares had made a spur-of-the-moment career change and were now trying their luck at the bottom of the Andaman Sea.) Tired from the journey, Nina was staggering more than usual. Simon, who had a thick layer of white ointment plastered around his mouth to soothe his eczema, looked like a miniature clown who'd forgotten half his make-up. As for me, I'd been growing a rather archaic-looking beard ever since my €99 razor exploded on Ko Phra Thong; I was foolish enough to plug it into what looked like a perfectly harmless electric socket. I'd tried to compensate by wearing my least-battered T-shirt, but you couldn't know that if you weren't acquainted with the rest of my wardrobe. Then there was the sand. We'd given up the struggle against it weeks before, finally accepting it as an inevitable part of our lives. Since then it had seeped into every crevice of our existence, and it trickled out from unexpected places at the slightest movement. We left a trail of grains in our wake wherever we went.

We were also in a conspicuously good mood. There was nothing sophisticated, elegant or dignified about this mood. It wasn't a mood suitable for a palace; it was almost improperly boisterous. Anyone seeing us arrive at the Prince Palace might have taken us for a troop of court jesters and fools that had come to remind the king of the vanity and transience of earthly existence with our jokes and tricks.

I imagined Curitiba Man sitting businesslike in his tailored suit in the hotel lounge. (Since adopting more than a passing resemblance to Cro-Magnon Man, I had begun to think of my former self in this way.) I imagined him catching sight of this band of jesters and breaking off his career-enhancing informal talk to stutter and stare. And I pictured my Cro-Magnon self going over to offer him a juggling ball, in the same way that the jester outside the Conference of the Parties in Brazil had approached me. 'You want try? Your turn!'

Mr Simon would stare wide-eyed at the high-flyer through his clown's mask. And my former self would recoil a step to restore that crucial professional distance and shake his head, murmuring to himself, 'How could they let themselves go like that?'

Perhaps most essential to our metamorphosis was the change to living in the now. It had started with Nina's 'really nice things' on Ko Phra Thong – all the games we played, all those excursions into the paradise of childhood. If top corporate managers could let it all hang out, then we certainly could. But it took a while. I remember the day on Ko Yao Yai when I went under the open-air shower in my shorts and T-shirt for the first time, then let my cool, wet clothes dry on my skin on the moped ride home. Lovely. We had spent seven weeks on the beach before I finally managed to follow Nina's example and relax enough to lie down with my head on the sand. Yes, you get a lot of sand in your hair. Yes, it's true, it doesn't all come out, even in the shower. But you get to sink in, deeper and deeper, like something gently washed ashore that gradually becomes one with the beach.

Flip-flops change the way you walk, and how fast you walk. If you can't slow down, you end up with some nasty chafing. *No stresstic* becomes a matter of course.

Another thing that helped me to change was not having a mirror (or as I referred to it, having a non-mirror). Without a mirror, a crucial link to your ego is broken; it stops receiving information and you begin to forget that you ever had a reflection. Great. I thought Vera had never looked so beautiful. Her hair in the wind. No make-up. Her eyes shining happily in her tanned face. No unnecessary clothes or accessories. No jewellery. Her feet bare. And the kids? They finally looked as wild as they were!

Interestingly, children don't need as many possessions as grown-ups. To begin with, only one thing really matters: *mama*. But gradually, more and more things become important, and the more there are, the shorter their useful half-life. Walking around the big toyshop with Nina as my consultant had always been a highlight in Bonn.

On our travels, all that changed. The few toys we'd brought with us stayed at the bottom of the suitcase, as if we'd only brought them because they couldn't be left on their own all that time. New toys were as rare as electricity from the plug sockets. The only things we bought – and frequently replaced – were plastic spades and balls. You can't do without a ball, we soon discovered. Superglue was handy too, to repair our few essentials. You need large quantities of superglue when your 69kg have to travel a million minutes.

Over the months, we got used to waiting for things to find us. There are more things around than you'd think, and we got into the habit of converting random objects into toys or climbing frames or furniture. Our world began to consist increasingly of jetsam – random objects we'd find lying on the beach in the morning. They had once been part of a boat or a container, but now they were fragments without a place or purpose. These things had been washed away, and after aimless drifting had run aground in the middle of our journey. In the hands of the children, they were given new meaning and became part of a new story, and for a while they were rafts or ships, bridges or houses – until, in the end, they went missing or reverted to being expendable remnants, once more stripped of meaning by weather and time and chance, and returned for who knows how long to the tide of anonymity. I added *jetsam-gatherer* to the list of potential jobs in my journal.

\* \* \*

There was no jetsam in the Prince Palace, everything there was solid and designed to be permanent. We planned to stop drifting for a couple of nights and tidy ourselves up a bit. Our plane to Australia left the evening after next, and the Aussie immigration authorities are famous for behaving like guards at the gates of heaven trying to keep out an army of charging Vandals. Even applying for Australian visas had been a full-time, full-on job that had kept us busy for weeks. We'd provided bank statements, got good at ignoring sarcastic comments to our garbled responses to incomprehensible questions, submitted health certificates and filled in a 100-plus-page form, on which we were expected to give personal reasons for choosing to visit Australia. For *each of us individually*, that is. The immigration officers could be glad they hadn't had to question us one by one; they'd have been pretty surprised at some of the things Nina had to tell them. Anyway, having gone to all that trouble, it seemed a shame to screw up at border control, and Vera and I had decided it would be best if we could at least *look* like ordinary people when we landed in Cairns. So that was our reason for booking in to the five-star Palace, where there was laundry service, a huge array of cosmetic products, bathrooms with mirrors and even a vast hotel supermarket, with several floors worth of all those everyday commodities we had left behind. Now, for a few hours, they caught up with us.

For Nina and Mr Simon it was only another world, another adventure playground. Unintimidated by the grave pomp of the place, they soon created their own interpretations of what they found. If half an old door lying on a beach was a raft, a heavy leather sofa in a hotel lobby was a trampoline – or at least it would be if the business people, those *serious people in black clothes*, as Nina called them, would budge up a bit. A reproduction Ming vase, hung with a sign of a crossed-out hand in a red circle, was perfect for hiding behind. Peacock feathers couldn't possibly be there just to look at – and what a stroke of luck that the beanbags by the pool were slowly leaking little polystyrene balls that the wind blew in little eddies across the terrace. With a small index finger you could even enlarge the hole, creating two or three eddies at a time – and soon the swimming pool looked as if it had been in a snowstorm. The swimming pool cleaner robot, meanwhile, sucked in bananas as if he'd never tasted anything so delicious. I used up an entire tube of superglue fixing what the children had unwittingly broken, mending things I didn't mention even to Vera. I also had to apologise to a nice, softly spoken man in Palace uniform who took me aside for a quiet word. No, no, I assured him, he was right, good behaviour was definitely important (in theory, anyway).

Only one thing rather spoilt my jetsam theory: Nina had fallen in love with the semi-precious cabbage on the plinth in Tower Two. The day we had arrived, she stopped in the middle of a furious game of tag and stared at it, awestruck.

'A lettuce,' she said excitedly. 'Is it a lettuce?'

'Looks like it,' I said drily.

'It's so beautiful!' She stroked it admiringly. 'Feel how smooth it is.'

'It's actually a cabbage made of jade,' I said. 'A green semi-precious stone.'

'Can I take it?'

'Try and pick it up,' I said.

Nina pulled at the colossal brassica, hesitantly at first and then harder. Nothing happened. Eventually she mustered all her energy and leant into it from underneath with her shoulder. The cabbage didn't budge a millimetre; 20 Ninas wouldn't have shifted the thing.

'You're not helping me at all,' she said with a red face.

'I prefer to help you think,' I said.

'Pff,' she said. She wasn't so easily deterred. 'I'll just have to practise a bit.'

'Even if you could lift it, do you think it would fit in your rucksack?' I asked, but got no reply.

The afternoon before our flight she begged me for permission to pay one last visit to the *lettuce*. I braced myself for protracted farewells.

But there was no drama; a bare five minutes later, Nina returned.

'So you're OK about leaving the lettuce?' I asked, surprised.

'It's staying here,' she said serenely.

She was, she added, pretty sure that it would have been possible to get a small tuk-tuk into the big service lift, and failing that there were always helicopters, flying dogs or dragons. But she'd decided not to bother with the lettuce after all.

That's my girl. I heard fanfares and drumrolls inside my head. I was proud. Nina was on the right track. Only five years old, and already she had recognised the limitations of giant semi-precious vegetables; maybe she'd even grasped the idea of downsizing. The million-minute journey was beginning to pay off.

'Bit *too* heavy, eh?' I hazarded.

'No, no,' she said. 'It tasted too dusty.'

# SHORTCUT TO SOMEDAY

WE ARRIVED IN AUSTRALIA WITHOUT FURTHER ADO. Our plane landed in Cairns in the middle of the night and even the most conscientious airport worker didn't feel like carrying out thorough checks at that hour, not on two exhausted and rather oddly attired figures plus shrieking baby plus argumentative little girl armed with a rucksack full of precious shells and a length of driftwood.

After waiting five hours for our relaxed car hire man to open up his shop half an hour late and then vanish again to get himself a coffee, we headed north. During the three months' island-hopping in Thailand, we'd moved around quite often. Here in Australia, we wanted a base where we could stay put a little longer. On the northernmost stretch of the Australian east coast, in the part of Queensland known as the Tropical North, summer was beginning. Here, after following the coast for thousands of miles, the mountains of the Great Dividing Range peter out into foothills that reach almost to the sea, and the clouds driven east across the land get caught in the mountains and melt. The result is dense tropical rainforest – and beyond the rainforest, brilliant blue sky stretching out over the largest coral reef in the world.

Tourists who make the marathon journey up the coast from Sydney tend to be happy to stay in Cairns, too knackered to go on, and few of them venture further north. Our plan was to head for Port Douglas, and it turned out to be a good idea. We rented a small house that nobody wanted because the owner had only recently managed to evict a bad-tempered, metre-and-a-half-long crocodile from its swimming pool. Nina was rather sorry about this, but the uncertain whereabouts of the crocodile gave her cause for hope. Nobody knew where the reptile was now. Had it ended up in the kitchen of a posh restaurant or slipped off the back of the pickup truck at the first bend in the road? Or had it perhaps been set free by a soft-hearted nature-lover? But the house was a mere 400 metres from the beach where, as Nina was thrilled to discover, you might – if you were *really lucky* – come across free-roaming crocs any day of the week (crocodiles have been fully protected in Queensland since 1974). In the playground on Solander Boulevard, there was even a sign low enough for a child to read: *Beware of the crocodiles!* Maybe not the best place for unsupervised play. But we were happy to take the hazardous property in Morning Close at a discount 'without liability'. The estate agents could be happy, too: as long as there were no further incidents, the dust would have settled on the croc story by the time we left in four or five months, and the next tenants could be charged full whack.

We spent a lot of afternoons at one of Port Douglas's attractions, Wildlife Habitat, as we had bought an annual family pass. Nina had found a hole in the wooden box where the feed pellets for some of the animals were stored; it was a win-win situation for all involved, except the company who managed the place. My duty was to sit on a bench and ignore what was going on, but to whistle loudly if anyone approached. This apparently unmotivated whistling must have struck people as odd, but I got quite a bit of reading done.

I had recently started on the comic strip *Calvin and Hobbes*, as someone had pointed out to me that Nina's behaviour bore an uncanny resemblance to that of Calvin, the little boy. Although Hobbes wasn't a flying dog but a speaking tiger, I wondered if Bill Watterson had been inspired by some kind of being like Nina, who –

as Finkelbach had put it – rigorously refused to distinguish between fiction and reality. When I showed her some of the comics she said that Calvin had really great ideas and that she would definitely try to meet him.

*    *    *

Nina's boundless generosity quickly promoted her to the role of world's best animal keeper. The kangaroos and emus of Port Douglas will be reminiscing about the good old days with the little blonde girl for years to come, thanks to the tonnes of extra pellets *kindly provided by the hole in the box*, as Nina put it. Five and a half months into our journey, we could hardly, any of us, have been happier.

Another favourite pastime was going on expeditions to the rainforest. We had only to walk about ten minutes from Mossman Gorge car park and another 100 metres or so into Daintree National Park and then we were in a world of towering rainforest trees with buttress roots as high as a room, twisting lianas, strangler figs choking the trees with their deadly skeletons, glow-in-the-dark fungi and tree frogs that looked as if they'd been dreamt up by an acid casualty. Branches bowed under the weight of treetop ferns, and we saw armies of giant ants, carnivorous plants and the last surviving specimens of the endangered southern cassowary – an enormous flightless bird with a shimmering blue neck. For Nina, all this was incontrovertible proof that flying dogs were nothing out of the ordinary.

Winding through this burgeoning lushness were rivers whose cool water was so clean we could probably have drunk it. Water is a precious resource in Australia, but here it tumbled into glittering, rocky basins of bubbling blue-green, snaked its way past huge, smooth polished rocks, surged under giant fallen trees and vanished into the steaming undergrowth.

There aren't many rainforests on earth suitable for children – and I'd seen a few in my time – but this one, a Garden of Eden, was an absolute delight. We had a number of favourite destinations for our adventures: the far side of the torrent, the deep unexplored forest, the country beyond the mysterious mountains, the land of the giant trees and the magic whirlpools. The latter were natural basins washed into the rocks – swimming pools in the middle of the rainforest! (Fortunately, the mountain spring water is too cold for crocs.) One aspect of their magic was that you couldn't swim in them without getting ravenously hungry, and when that happened, meatballs, sandwiches and chicken drumsticks would appear on our picnic rug as if magicked up by fairies. That's how Vera put it, while secretly filling our backpacks like Father Christmas. As far as the children were concerned, this fairy picnic was all part of the show.

Today, the four of us found lozenge-shaped rolls with goat's cheese and tomatoes and mangos. Everything was just right: the forest had cooled down a little, but was still warm enough for us to sit around after our swim without shivering – and the mosquitos wouldn't get going for another hour or so. Water dripped out of my hair onto the forest floor. It was a perfect moment. Nothing to do but relax and enjoy. No need to move. No need to think.

'What do you want to be when you grow up?'

'Eh?' It was as much as I could manage to balance the tomatoes on my roll.

'When you're big! What do you want to be?' Nina insisted.

Someone had probably asked her the day before. Children are always being asked. Grown-ups throw the question at them a good 15 years before they can make proper decisions of their own. I suppose adults have this yen to hear dreamy answers, unfettered by reality. Later on, when life gets serious, they stop asking. But this was typical. This kind of question could come from Nina at any time – from beneath a cloud of bubble bath, or out of the darkness of a restless night, in the last seconds of a phone call I'd thought was over, or at the supermarket checkout with the cashier scanning the shopping twice as fast as I could fill the bags. Each time – like now, on this sunny afternoon in the middle of the rainforest in the Tropical North – I was caught off guard.

I asked *her* the question, to buy time. 'What about you?'

'Fireman, of course,' she said. 'And I want to fly.'

Flying was something we practised regularly: I'd throw her in the air, as high as I could, while she tried to spread her 'wings' in the short time before I caught her again. But the fireman idea was new.

'Fire*woman*?'

'Yes.' But she wasn't to be distracted. 'Tell me!'

'Um, I'll have to think about it.'

\*   \*   \*

What *did* I want to be when I grew up? For me, it was a retrospective question. After all, I *was* grown up. When I was little, I'd have answered like a shot. For as long as I could remember, I'd dreamt of travelling around the world. I had dreams of sailing on all the different oceans, climbing in the Andes and the Himalayas, trekking over wastes of ice in Alaska, through the Amazon rainforest and across the desert. I longed to see the Seven Wonders of the World, to visit exotic countries – Borneo, Egypt, Japan – and of course I wanted to go to Australia, the land of no horizon, and see the Aboriginals.

'I want to do all that!' I told my paternal grandad one wishful morning, standing in the corner of the sandpit, where he'd set me down so he could have a smoke.

'That's not a profession,' he grumbled. Grandad Hans evidently had little time for plans unfettered by reality. He was an industrial metalworker by trade; he had slogged away in the Ruhr Valley, and sometimes deep down under the earth. The WWII generation. Fighting against the Russians in the infamously bloody Battle of Stalingrad had changed him, Grandma always said. Then there was the bomb that was dropped on their little house and, as if that weren't enough, he'd lost his only son, my father, to the world of classical music. Now his grandson was prattling on about the wonders of the world. Grandad knew how it felt to go for days without having enough to eat, what it meant not to have the money for warm clothes. It was important to him that a man had a proper profession, one that would be sure to earn him a living. 'What *profession* will you choose, lad?'

'Round-the-world traveller,' I replied timidly. It wasn't quite the right term – even I realised that – but I wanted Grandad Hans to understand that I was at least as serious about the matter as he was. In fact, I had no intention of travelling non-stop. From what I'd gleaned from the books I'd read, those seafarers and explorers had a pretty gruelling time of it. Alexander von Humboldt, David Livingstone, Ernest Shackleton – their lives weren't exactly a walk in the park. What I wanted was to go and live in the far-off countries they had visited, discover exotic habits and customs, make friends, experience the strange and the wonderful – nothing strange and terrible, please.

'But round-the-world traveller isn't a real job,' my grandad mumbled, stubbing out his cigarette on the wooden frame of the sandpit with his brown stained thumb; and that was the end of it. In his eyes, I had somehow failed, maybe in rather the same way that Nina had failed with her flying dog answer. If he'd lived to see me reach the age of reason – or what he considered that to be – I dare say he'd have given me another chance. But he died young, and with no other relative intent on establishing what I wanted to be, I must have given up trying to find a more adequate way to describe my dream job.

So when I was a young child, I knew exactly what I wanted to do when I was an adult, but had no way of achieving it. Later, at university, I had phenomenal energy but rarely any money, being a typical student – though I did manage to get a semester ahead of myself so that Vera and I could go travelling in South America. When after graduation I started work as a tropical research scientist (sure that I'd found the perfect job) I spent 90% of my time sitting under the strip lighting in the institute, writing articles and proposals. Writing a proposal took weeks and theoretically allowed you to spend about the same amount of time travelling, but only if you were prepared to devote the rest of the year to producing scholarly articles to add to your publication list. My sumptuous UN grant meant that I was flown all over the place – Geneva, Rome, Nairobi – but rarely had more than half a day to look around at the end of each trip. (I suppose that's why a good third of the world's natural history collections are housed within 100km of an urban area, because most collectors didn't have the resources to get any further.) The PhD students at the institute in Bonn had a running joke: an angel appears to two research assistants and their supervisor, and grants each of them a wish. Research assistant number one wishes to be transported to a desert island with his girlfriend, and his wish comes true. Research assistant number two wishes to be snowed in in an Alpine hut; his wish comes true, too. And then their supervisor wishes to have the two of them back in the lab when lunch break's over.

Once I'd got my consultant job at the UN, money began to flow in, but I no longer had any leisure time; I worked up to 19 hours a day and then slept. Maybe in old age I'd have plenty of time and money, but by then I'd be fighting for my health, not my dreams.

If there's one sure-fire way never to realise your dreams, it's to wait for that *someday* when you have everything – energy *and* health *and* money *and* time *and* imagination. I hadn't even noticed I was waiting. I had professional goals, of course: a professorship or a longer-term job at the UN. And I fantasised about owning a beautiful house and a shiny red car and taking a two-week luxury holiday every summer. It was the same for my friends, but our original childhood dreams? We'd put them on hold. *Someday.* Of course we'd get round to everything someday. But you had to be realistic. The trouble was that being realistic and putting off your dreams left *someday* looking pretty complicated. The day that you'd have everything at once, with enough money never to have to worry about your bank balance again. The odds for that are at least 75 million to one against – and that's assuming you play the lottery. Then you'll want to be in the pink of health, which takes the odds to about 300 million to one. No good being tied down by responsibilities either, so ailing relatives are a no-no, ditto kids in dramatic teen relationships. Call it 500 million to one. Lastly, of course, you'll need infinite time, but since you're also supposed to be generating heaps of money, a normal job is out of the question. (This is something career advisors omit to tell you when you're 18.) The chances are, then, that you'll be wanting a new job too, preferably something vaguely criminal or involving the stock exchange. And because all these things have to happen at once, your overall chances of ever reaching that *someday* are about a billion to one against. Which is a bummer, because average life expectancy in the West is about 30,000 days. If you're set on being realistic, you might find yourself waiting 3,333 lives before you finally hit on the right day, and *someday* begins.

My friend Anna Amsel once said that life is like doing a drawing with only one piece of paper and no rubber. I sometimes imagined my piece of paper. It would be full of loops and pointless scribbling, one-way streets and blind spots – quite beautiful in parts, but shot through with dark, cross-hatched patches where I'd got stuck or complacent. There would be false paths leading nowhere in particular, followed because they were seductive or convenient; and, past a certain point in my life, there would be an increasing number of paths I'd been travelling for so long that changing tack was almost unthinkable. A strategically planned career is more like a dot-to-dot picture where one thing leads to another, but it doesn't leave much scope for big dreams. There's only so much room on a piece of paper. Where were the dreams on mine? Is that the mistake we make? We forget to draw our dreams while there's still space for them? Replace them with those stupid to-do lists where the important things don't feature?

Then along came Nina, and later Simon, and all the routes I'd sketched in, all those fast lanes, had to be abandoned. Sorry mate, forget it. At first, I felt as if I'd come to the end of the line. But then something incredible happened: the slip road I had been so hesitant to take turned out to be a shortcut to someday. Soon after Nina's million-minute idea, I began to replot my dreams on that metaphorical piece of paper – only a few tentative dots to begin with, but there they were: it was a beginning. What do you really want to do? What do you actually want to be? I had a daughter with an insatiable appetite for adventure, a wife who was happy to travel to the end of the world with me and a baby son who didn't mind what he did as long as nobody woke him too early in the morning. We had the money from the middle-of-the-range new car we hadn't bought and the loan money for the carport I hadn't built and the furniture we would never buy. And we knew that normal life wasn't going to work for us. So what were we waiting for?

Putting your dreams down on that piece of paper is almost the same as realising them.

Our realistic friends and family produced argument after argument against our proposal, and it was clear that we were going to have to perform an enormous miracle if we wanted to make this 'so-unrealistic' journey happen.

The time-lapse version went like this:

Vera organised po-faced passport photos of the kids (no smiles allowed). I explained to worried grandparents that it was basically a very long holiday. We had the kids vaccinated against 11 and a half diseases. (Best if the doctor holds the baby, or the poor little thing will feel betrayed. No discount for inoculating children? Oh well.) Of course they have nappies out there, or some approximation to them. No, the rocking horse isn't going to starve. Vomex is best for puking. My pension? No, this isn't going to improve it. Did you know you can get snake-venom pumps second-hand? Of course I'll send you a postcard! Two pairs of trousers, max. I had my email address printed inside the kids' T-shirts – a weird feeling. Pippi Longstocking tapes, hmm… Visit us? Sure, any time! Spare glasses for Nina. A bit big? Good, that's the idea – she'll grow into them. I'll miss you too. That? You can have that – don't think I'm going to be needing it. No, really, the painkillers are only for emergencies. Superglue? You bet! Comes with a little brush these days – 'for greater precision'. Sunscreen factor 50 – seriously?

After about 55 full-on days, we were through the worst of it and on the way to realising our dreams. I never thought I'd end up on good terms with to-do lists, but these were the loveliest I'd ever made. I headed these lists *The Journey, Lonely Island* and *Valley of the Giants*.

Right up to the second the plane took off from Bonn, I was afraid we'd be thwarted by some aspect of so-called *reality*. But the plane rumbled and lifted into the sky. And here we finally were. In the middle of Queensland's rainforest. In the middle of my big dream. Our big dream.

\* \* \*

'This is what I want to be!' I almost shouted the words; it had only that instant become clear to me.

'Eh?' Now it was Nina's turn to be confused. While I had been pondering my life, she'd been busy diverting a thousand-strong trail of worker ants. They were still a little bemused. I wondered where their slip road off the motorway of life would take them.

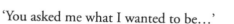

'You asked me what I wanted to be...'

'Yes,' she said, still busy with the ants.

'Well, what I'm saying is that I want to be just what I am now. Here we are with all this time and the rainforest and our expeditions. We can go snorkelling by the reef and walking in the mountains. We're discovering things every day. Simon's learning to walk on the beach. I always wanted to be a...' There it was again – that missing word for what I wanted to be. Strictly speaking, of course, I was unemployed, generating no income. Grandad Hans would turn in his grave if he could see how his grandson had turned out. 'I want this.'

And the lovely thing was that Nina knew what I meant.

'I see,' she said simply, diverting another section of the ant trail. My announcement clearly came as no surprise to her. She couldn't know that it had taken me decades to get this far. She'd probably have found it incomprehensible if I'd told her there were people who didn't ever get round to realising any of their dreams.

'We still have to do the ceremony!' she said in a slightly demanding tone.

Earlier, I'd promised that we would pretend we'd discovered a new country and mark our conquest with a little ceremony, but all that thinking had left me in a state of turmoil. It's not every day that you realise you're in the middle of your life's dream.

'All right then.' I climbed onto a fallen tree trunk, threw my hands to the bright sky with a dramatic flourish and prepared to hold forth.

'Wait!' Nina said, climbing onto another trunk. 'OK, now! I grant you a speech.' She motioned to me with her hand.

Mr Simon, sitting on Vera's lap, chuckled.

'Well then. Yes. Here we are. We've reached this new country. After months of travelling.' My humorous speech was making me feel slightly queasy. I wasn't in the mood for joking about. I was so happy I felt like crying. 'We have swum through torrents, traversed dangerous forests, conquered eerie, mist-swathed peaks.' I was hamming it up, trying to make them laugh. But I couldn't shake this funny feeling.

I cleared my throat. 'We've seen so much already.' I took an unnecessarily deep breath. 'We have left many things behind us to journey into the unknown.' I actually had a lump in my throat. I caught Vera's eye. 'And now we've made it.'

I smiled, choking up. 'All this way!' I tried to get a grip on myself, but my sentences were getting shorter and shorter. I'd never have thought a wave of emotion would hit me so suddenly, not in the middle of some silly speech. Vera put Simon down on the rug and came over to embrace me.

'Dear faithful...' I still hadn't found the right word. 'Dear...'

'Adventure people?' Nina suggested.

# FISHERMAN, FISHERMAN, HOW DEEP IS THE WATER?

320,000TH MINUTE
PORT DOUGLAS (16°48'S, 145°46'E)
TROPICAL NORTH QUEENSLAND, AUSTRALIA

'DO YOU THINK I'LL EVER BE ABLE TO DO IT?'

Nina was lying on the grass in Port Douglas's Anzac Park, covered in fine pale sand. It was on her T-shirt and in her hair and all over one side of her face, which was streaked with rivulets of tears.

'Come here, let's help you up,' I said, holding out my hand. Then I decided that was a little too indulgent – after all, it wasn't a big deal – and added more breezily, 'Get up, if you're a Nina!'

That was what Nina's childminder Gabi had always said, and the words usually drew a smile from her when nothing else would. Gabi, a wonderful soul, was a dedicated fan of the German football team FC Schalke 04, who knew all about falling down and getting up again. Apparently, 'Get up if you're a Schalker' was what the crowd yelled at the team when they were losing 0–2 and playing in driving rain with only 18 minutes to go. The magic words rarely let me down; they were a sticking plaster for Nina's soul. But today the panacea didn't work. Lying there in the brilliant sunshine, she was a picture of misery.

Anzac Park is at the northernmost tip of Port Douglas and ends in a large, almost circular peninsula edged with tall palms and other trees. (The playground is about 50 metres inland, so that children aren't right next to the open water.) All around us, kids were running about, men were barbecuing and women were pushing buggies. There were a few office workers with loosened ties enjoying a short break, a handful of tourists and the mandatory surfers with their waxed boards and tipsy groupies with the kind of drinks it's wisest to avoid if you intend to get any surfing done.

During our months in Port Douglas, we spent a lot of time in that park – except for the quarter of an hour between about 6:15 and 6:30 in the evening, when the bats and flying foxes left town in their thousands, to fly back to their woods and caves. If you hung around at that time, you stood a good chance of being hit by something wet falling from the sky.

We got an unintended glimpse of the flying show on our fourth day in Port Douglas. Nina was playing with another child on the climbing frame when she saw it, and wheeled round to him.

'Flying foxes,' he explained with a shrug.

I flinched. But the question was on its way to me before I had the chance to prepare.

'Daddy, what does the word *fox* mean?' She was making sure of her ground before launching her attack.

'I guess it means *Fuchs*,' I admitted.

'You lose!' she cried triumphantly. 'Foxes are dogs, aren't they?'

'I guess you could say that foxes and dogs are related.' Something told me it wouldn't be easy to get out of this one. 'But in German,' I added, 'fruit bats happen to be called *flying dogs*, not *flying foxes* as they are in Australia.'

Nina's eyes grew bigger. She drew breath to speak, but I hastened to explain that these huge bats weren't *real* dogs.

'Why not?'

I searched frantically for an answer. As far as I could remember, bats and flying foxes were only distant phylogenetic relations. It would have to do.

'Because in Australia, fruit bats are called flying foxes, not dogs.'

Nina's eyebrows shot up again. Like the redundant English word *flittermouse*, the German word for a microbat – *Fledermaus* – makes some bats sound like a species of mouse. She laughed at me. 'And tomorrow there'll be flying cats – especially for you, Daddy!'

I was about to say something like, 'You have a wonderful imagination,' but then I recalled those green monkeys, a species of blue-testicled vervet, that not only leap through the treetops almost as if flying but also, confusingly, are known in German as meerkats: *Grüne Meerkatzen*. There was no knowing what we'd come across next. I bit my lip. Nina laughed again and went back to her climbing. She never bore grudges.

\* \* \*

On this particular day, Vera and I had arranged to meet some of our new friends in the park. Will had settled on a rock, as usual, and was watching people amusing themselves and picnicking on the grass, while Jackie was busy stretching his slackline between two palms without damaging their bark. Nearby, Jesse and Robby were rehearsing for a performance at next Sunday's craft market. Now and then, the shimmering tones of Jesse's hang drum drifted over to us.

Since coming to the park, Nina and I had started to play our own variation of the German children's game 'Fisherman, fisherman, how deep is the water?' The aim was to cross the 15-metre 'ocean' between Jackie's palm trees and the climbing frame in as original a way as possible, and that morning we had crossed it skipping sideways like a crab, crawling, and then finally hopping. No one was 'it' when we played, except maybe Mr Simon, who had learned to walk on Port Douglas's Four Mile Beach and, to Nina's irritation, sometimes took it upon himself to enter the 'ocean' and throw himself at her as she struggled with whatever special movement was called for. The game had come about more or less by chance, but I had seized on it gratefully, as I could generally be sure of sneaking in a bout of motor-skills training with Nina. This game was important for both of us. Where else could she practise the things that took her so much longer to learn than other children, if not here? Our million-minute journey had given us both the time and the place – many ideal places – for Nina to thrive.

The downside was that it often put us in a bad mood and regularly ended in tears, like now. Nina was very determined and, in a way, this particular boot camp was self-inflicted. But like every child, she had her limits. Halfway through trying to hop across the 'ocean', she'd toppled over for the third time and had given up. Now she was sitting beside me, sobbing.

Vera came over, carrying Mr Simon. 'I think she's had enough,' she said quietly.

'We're only practising. We'll try again in a second,' I replied.

Vera looked at me sternly. 'Is this a game you're playing together or is it some personal project of yours?'

She'd touched a nerve.

'Rubbish,' I said.

'You were driving her quite hard just now.'

'I'll never manage!' wailed a small voice beside me. 'I'll never be able to join the fire brigade, will I? Ever!' Nina knew she could lay it on a bit thicker now that Vera had joined us.

I tried not to show my frustration. Without thinking through what he was saying, a neighbour of ours had told Nina all about the fire brigade – what you had to be able to do to join up, and how they only took the fittest of the fit. (It was, he said, the same with the police.) Since then, Nina had made it her mission to climb as high as she could, slide down the firefighter's pole on the playground, run fast, carry heavy objects and so on. Our game on the grass had become a way of testing herself for her prospective career.

This fire-brigade business gnawed away at me. Nina didn't even have three-dimensional vision. If she tried to light a candle, she sometimes held the extra-long match too far from the wick as she waited patiently for it to catch. There was the list of Greek words on her medical report to take into account – and then of course, Nina being Nina, any firefighting career she had in mind would be transformed into a sensational circus show. Clear the ring! Today we bring you the unrivalled local fire brigade with the magic rescue-net trampoline, a high-pressure water fight, the exploding giant hose-snake, a costume contest and a freely improvised pyrotechnic show – not forgetting all the sausages you can eat and pavement chalk for everyone. Roll up, roll up, come and marvel! No, it was more than likely that Nina's dream would never come true.

'Let's wait and see,' I said, not wanting to rob her of her dream. I'd rather she learned to fight than gave up too soon. But what should I say?

'You can get a long way in life if you fight for what you want,' I said, looking defiantly at Vera, who knew me well enough to realise that this wasn't the moment to try to re-educate me.

'Why don't the two of you fight it out in Café Origin while Nina has a hot chocolate?' she suggested. 'Sarah and I will start getting food ready and when you come back, we can have lunch.'

I glanced at Nina, whose face had brightened at the mere mention of hot chocolate. 'Yes, a break might be a good idea,' I agreed.

I was quite happy to be outmanoeuvred, but I didn't want to be seen to give way. Dealing with Nina's yearnings for goals that might always be beyond her reach was a constant challenge for me.

So we sauntered over to Origin, which was our favourite café and already a regular feature of our summer routine. The prospect of coffee and hot chocolate put a spring in our stride. Origin must have been one of the most relaxed cafés on the east coast of Australia; everyone there, employees and punters alike, was always in a good mood. Every morning, Glenn the barista would make a show of closing his eyes, sipping the first cup of the day and announcing in satisfied tones that today the coffee had turned out just the way he wanted. The hot chocolate was so chocolatey that you could stand a spoon in it. The children would happily have taken up residence in Café Origin.

Although it was a bit out on a limb and not really on the way to anywhere, we often found ourselves 'just passing'. It was also a good place for me to write my journal, read the papers and gradually get to know the other regulars. There was Jasmine, who earned a living giving Tarot card readings. Wages in Australia are at least half as high again as in Germany – even, it seems, for psychics and mediums – and Jasmine could live pretty well off two clairvoyant sessions a day (she charged extra for reading the future). I occasionally eavesdropped on these sessions – even though it was strictly forbidden – and when I heard the stories people offloaded, I decided that she more than deserved the money she made. Then there was Ron, a rather taciturn flight instructor for microlight aircraft. The first few times I saw him, he virtually goose-stepped into the café without looking left or right and immediately vanished behind a newspaper. But things changed a little once I'd been flying with him in his two-seater microlight – Vera's birthday present to me. When we reached 400 metres, Ron, ignoring my loud protests, handed over the controls, then sat with his arms folded across his chest while I endured two endless minutes of sweat and terror, but somehow managed not to kill us. He seemed to develop a certain fondness for me after that, and we even exchanged the odd word.

Sometimes in the afternoon we saw Sabrina, a beautiful restaurant chef from Portugal. Sabrina's dream had always been to cook for people who were genuinely hungry, but for years she'd had to resign herself to catering for wealthy tourists in expensive resorts, whose egos tended to be even bigger than their appetites. Now, thanks to her baby daughter Lou, who was always starving, she finally had her heart's desire. Lou had unabashedly made clear that she considered herself Mr Simon's first girlfriend. Maybe she thought he had beautiful eyes. The two of them spent many an afternoon passing sand moulds back and forth to each other, and Mr Simon was astonished to discover that one-year-old Portuguese-Australian girls seemed to regard snogging as an essential part of any decent friendship. I was reminded of my timid teenage years. Aged 16, and hardly more experienced than Mr Simon, I had approached a girl I liked and asked in several convoluted sentences whether it wouldn't perhaps, theoretically, be a good idea if we – provided of course that... Juli saw where I was headed and her reply was a model of clarity and concision: 'No.'

Only one person seemed out of place in the café: the jealous Héloise. She had a book café of her own that was barred to dogs, cats and children – a fact she explained to me after Nina had been brazen enough to lever a book carefully from one of the shelves. And it wasn't even a children's book! It seemed to us that she was desperate to discover the secret of the ever-wonderful atmosphere in Glenn's café and thought she would find it in his coffee-brewing formula. It never seemed to occur to her that people prefer to be with you if you're fun to be around.

Jim – blond, tanned, athletically built and endowed with an irresistible sense of humour – was pretty much the exact opposite. He specialised in seducing female Russian tourists, and pursued this programme several days a week, with considerable success. Origin was a safe haven for his preliminary moves, and he always made a big thing of showing his Russian ladies what good mates he was with everyone in the café. And fair to say, he *was* a very likeable bloke – always obliging and always ready with a joke on the rare occasions he came in on his own. The only time he lost his cool was when we asked him why he didn't go and sit with the jealous café owner for once. That really *was* going too far. She didn't even look Russian.

Then there was *the poor man*.

I'd seen him sitting at one of the outdoor tables a few times, but we'd never spoken and I hadn't noticed anything unusual about him. He wasn't there that morning when we arrived, but as we awaited our restorative hot drinks he appeared on an electric disability tricycle with a strange-looking trailer, the hum of his motor changing pitch depending on the speed. The man's face was weather-beaten, but there was something fragile-looking about his fine features, and his eyes were luminous. Smiling blithely, he cleared a broad path between the scattered chairs and manoeuvred his tricycle up to the table next to ours. Fitting into the tight space at the table was quite a feat: forwards, backwards, a little closer, forwards again, backwards – until at last he was more or less where he wanted to be. He must have had a portable radio in his trailer, because some absurd Monty Python tune was vying with the chart music coming from inside the café. Nina, ostentatiously inconspicuous, pulled my head down to her face with both hands and whispered, 'The poor man'.

He seemed to be part of the furniture; at any rate, most of the regulars greeted him with a friendly smile, and he didn't need to order the mug of coffee that Glenn brought him on a tray. 'Hi Michael,' he said. 'How's life today?'

Michael gave him a friendly nod. He had trouble getting the tray into position in front of him; even at the third attempt, it spun away from him on the freshly wiped table. But he observed this with a smile, as if it were somebody else's arm jerking and struggling with the thing.

'The poor man,' Nina repeated – a little louder, because I'd deliberately ignored her the first time.

'I think he's called Michael,' I said brusquely.

'He can't be a fireman, either.'

What a day… 'Nina, listen. You can do so many things. You just have to keep practising, and you'll get there in the end. No stresstic!' I did my best to sound upbeat.

'But what if I don't ever manage?'

'Some things have to go wrong a few times before they work out.' It didn't sound very convincing. 'Anyway,' I added, poking her in the ribs, 'you can always be the world's best animal keeper, can't you?'

What a stroke of genius. I was chuffed to see a small smile dart across her face. But it was short-lived; only a second later her face had clouded with worries again. It'll be a while before we solve this one, I thought, and I was glad when our glorious hot chocolate finally arrived and brightened her up a bit.

*   *   *

A few days later, Nina and I were sitting on Four Mile Beach playing Uno, a fairly fast-moving game because we'd supplemented our depleted pack with 19 wild cards made of sea-almond leaves. As we sat there, we heard the buzz of an electric motor mingled with snatches of Tom Waits – and who should appear in the distance but Michael, riding over the dunes.

'Oh, it's the poor man! What's he doing here?' Nina asked.

'He's not called the poor man,' I said firmly. 'He's called Michael. I've told you that. Please say *Michael*.'

'The poor man is called Michael,' she said stubbornly.

Michael gave us a cheery wave. We'd run into him a few times since that day in Origin. The electric motor struggled up the dunes towards us, then the front wheel tipped to one side and got stuck in the sand. End of the line for Michael, I thought, unsure whether to go over and help in case I caused offence. But Michael simply got off the tricycle and carried on. On his knees. On the ground. It was only now that I noticed cloth wrapped around each knee so he didn't chafe them on the ground. Awkwardly, he dragged himself around his trike, which I now realised was actually an adapted beach buggy, and pulled with all his strength at the thick aluminium frame of his trailer. It must have weighed 20kg or more. Nina and I watched in awed silence as he leant over it, breathing hard, tugging at a kind of tarpaulin or tent. More than once, the wind blew it around his body and he almost vanished beneath it; he also had trouble with the strings, which kept getting caught in the buggy. But he was immensely patient and eventually had the fluttering chaos under control. Now I could see that it wasn't a tent, but a big stunt kite. At last, Michael sat down in the sand.

Nina looked at me wide-eyed, but still said nothing as Michael laid the kite bundle on his lap, pushed his fists into the sand, almost to his wrists and propelled himself *backwards*, away from the buggy. You could see the muscles bulging beneath his T-shirt. Michael left a trail in the sand on his way to the sea: two fist prints every 30 centimetres, and between each set of prints a kind of furrow where he'd dragged his legs along. It was almost like the tracks left by the giant turtles we sometimes saw on the beach in the mornings. And he was moving backwards. Just watching him was tiring. Most fitness trainers would have given up by now – flung themselves, sobbing, onto the sand. But Michael battled on quietly and tenaciously. The strings of the stunt kite must have been about 15 metres long. Fisherman, fisherman, how deep is the water?

Unfathomably deep.

Nina still hadn't said anything, but had pressed herself close to me. It took Michael a good five minutes to position the kite near the waterline, flat on its back, the strings taut, and it was several more minutes before he could return to the buggy to slide back into the seat and manoeuvre his legs into the straps under the handlebars. His ribcage rose and fell as he gently began to pull the strings so that the kite could fill with air and unfold. There must have been five square metres of kite, I reckoned – probably impossible to hold the thing without a harness. The buggy shifted sideways as Michael struggled with the rod-shaped handle that held the strings. A jolt went through his sinuous torso and the buggy rolled forwards a few metres. Then another jolt, stronger this time, and the kite traced a figure of eight in the sky. The buggy rolled faster towards us and turned inland, really gathering pace now. Faster and faster. The wheels began to rattle, the kite whizzed through the air and sand sprayed on both sides as he shot past us in the buggy, propelled by the kite. And faster. We watched his progress, rapt. Eventually Michael was hurtling along the beach at an insane speed – way over 50km an hour. Sometimes the buggy scarcely seemed to touch the ground, and when it turned, it balanced alarmingly on two wheels, only slowing briefly before careering off again.

Still Nina said nothing. I realised in astonishment that she hadn't spoken a word since Michael had appeared on the beach. This had to be a record. She maintained this silence all the way home. But the nearer we got, the more quickly she walked.

When we reached the veranda, she ran straight into the kitchen and at last it all came gushing out. 'Mum, we saw Michael!'

'Who's Michael?' Vera asked, turning to me.

'The poor man,' I replied laconically.

Vera looked at me, but I wasn't given a chance to explain. Nina was chattering away excitedly, as if I hadn't spoken. 'Michael's a racing driver! With a kite! It's amazing. He can almost fly! On a tricycle. It's true! We went to the beach and played Uno and then…'

I closed the veranda door and the high-pitched voice faded away. Through the tinted glass, I could see Nina standing in front of Vera, gesticulating wildly, describing the sensation we had just observed on the beach, in minute detail.

At length, the door opened and Vera came and sat next to me.

'What do we do now?' she asked.

'What do you mean?' I said, knowing exactly what she meant.

'She's dead set on being a firefighter – in spite of everything.'

'I know. But it's good for her to learn to fight for her dreams, isn't it?'

Part of me felt helpless. There was a blind spot in my behavioural make-up. I knew how to fight. Always had. I couldn't accept it when people told me something wasn't doable – like our million-minute journey. But I knew, too, that there was another, less positive side to my fighting spirit.

That evening I opened my journal. There it was: *adventure people*, the term Nina had used a couple of months back. And on the same day, a little further down, I had scribbled: *It's important to fight for our dreams!* Now, beside it in the margin, I wrote: *If you want to learn how to sail, you have to set sail. But what about dreams that can't come true?*

# MICHAEL AND THE LIGHTNESS OF BEING

322,000TH MINUTE
PORT DOUGLAS (16°48'S, 145°46'E)
TROPICAL NORTH QUEENSLAND, AUSTRALIA

WATCHING MICHAEL SET UP HIS KITE ON THE BEACH, I had resolved to tell him how impressed I was. Maybe I would also mention how impressed Nina had been; after all, this was really about her. I decided to drop into Origin the next morning. I had an hour or two to spare because it was Nina's sixth birthday and she was keen to get to playgroup nice and early, as there was a little party planned with the other children. We were glad to have found a group for her in Port Douglas where the kids could cool off under a garden hose when it got hot – the mercury sometimes rose well above 30 degrees – and also where Mr Simon could join her if he wanted. The two of them had made plenty of friends, not forgetting Lou. That was particularly important to us after Thailand, where they hadn't had much of a chance to play with other children.

On the way to Origin, I began to have second thoughts. I had persuaded myself that Michael would be pleased with a compliment, but no one came up to me and congratulated me for getting on my bike, did they? What exactly was I after?

Whatever it was, I couldn't turn back now, as half the Origin crew had already spotted me. Glenn looked up from scrubbing a table and gave me a wave, and Jasmine threw me a look of warning to tell me she was busy with a customer. I noticed it was the woman with the short-cropped white hair who'd poured out her heart to her only the week before. It seemed the world was full of people desperate to unburden themselves.

Michael was there, too, his trike parked next to the table as usual. I sat down at a neighbouring table and saw him reach for his mug; some of the coffee slopped onto his jerky hand. A smile. Then a growl of satisfaction as he took his first gulp. Spilt coffee ran down the mug and dripped onto his thigh. I had to fight the impulse to take a napkin and mop the drip. I couldn't take my eyes off it. Suddenly I realised that Michael was watching me stare at him. What eyes he had! They were a brilliant aquamarine.

'Good morning,' he said in an unfamiliar accent. It was the first time I'd heard him speak. His eyes shone even more than usual, and his laughter lines appeared. As they faded, I noticed that the skin in between the lines was paler.

'Good morning, Michael,' I said, but it came out a little too fast, and I felt caught out despite his friendliness.

He said something else. It must have been 'How are you?' but it didn't really sound like it. The vowels were drawled and the consonants seemed to echo in his mouth.

'Fine, thanks. How are you?' I gave him a big nod, so he didn't have to go to the trouble of shaking my hand.

'Thanks, I'm great!' He held out his hand anyway and although I have quite big hands, mine vanished in his enormous paw like a child's. His handshake reminded me of my grandad's vice. (When I was a child, I used to like going down to the cellar in my grandparents' house and clamping my hand in that vice. There was a lovely smell of wood and glue down there, and sawdust on the floor that clung to my socks. I would carefully turn the wooden handle with my free hand until the diamond pattern on the metal blocks had etched itself into the ball of my thumb.) Everything about Michael was large and powerful. I could see every muscle cord in his athletic upper arms and recalled the way he had pushed himself along on his fists the day before.

'What's your name?' he asked politely, and I realised I hadn't introduced myself, even though I'd called him by his first name. He didn't seem bothered.

'I'm Wolf,' I said. 'Hi.' I still felt awkward and the best follow-up question I could manage was, 'What are you up to?'

It was an absurd question. What did I think the guy was up to? Michael looked at me quizzically and began to laugh. He laughed so much I was afraid the cough might prevail, but the laughter won out.

'I guess I'm having my coffee.' He gave me a little punch on the shoulder in that jerky slow-mo of his. That broke the ice. But if Michael's lightness was compelling, it was also confusing. It seemed impossible that this was the man I had watched drag himself through the sand the day before, centimetre by centimetre. Then we looked at each other and I, too, started to laugh at myself. It felt good.

*   *   *

Michael had gone out in the boat, he told me, the same as he did every day, and he was in the waters off Port Lincoln when it happened, down in the south of Australia, about 30 nautical kilometres from the coast. It was a clear, sunny day – 'just like today', Michael said – and there was a moderate swell. It was possible that the virus had already been in his body for a few days, undetected; the incubation period for the viral encephalitis that he experienced is about five days. And unless you happen to be a doctor and realise what's going on, you have little chance of reacting quickly enough once symptoms appear. Michael was a fisherman. The rest of the crew teased him at first, when he complained of a strange queasiness and an unfamiliar dizzy feeling. From the first signs that something wasn't right, it was only half an hour before paralysis set in. By the time they carried him ashore three hours later, he could no longer turn his head properly and barely had control of his hands. The encephalitis had attacked the nerve endings in his brain stem and begun its devastating work. Only 12 hours later, Michael had lost control of much of his body. He also had to jettison all his plans for the future; never again would he be able to make a living as a fisherman.

Michael didn't overdramatise or downplay his story. He simply gave me a brief report of the facts, his account of an incident that had occurred some time ago.

'You wanted to know, right?' he said with a gentle smile, when he saw the look on my face. 'But don't let my story get to you. Here we are, sitting in the sunshine on a beautiful day.'

His words echoed in my ears. There was no rancour or bitterness in them, and I could tell that he meant every word. I cradled my mug in my hands and for a while we both sipped our coffee in silence.

Then I remembered what I'd wanted to say to him.

'We saw you yesterday. I wanted to tell you how impressed I was by the way you set up the kite.'

'Thanks, that's nice of you.' He smiled, fixing me with his eyes. His face was perfectly frank and open. Other people let you see them only through tinted glass, or are always playing a role. But with Michael, I had the feeling that he let me look right inside him.

'Did you want to ask me something?' he said.

'Not really.' I felt something lurch inside me. Only a moment before, I'd been wondering what it was I wanted from him. I assumed a tone of self-deprecation. 'I think I just wanted to get off my chest how impressed I was. We saw you fighting, every inch of the way.'

'It's important to fight…' he said slowly.

Exactly, I said to myself, you must fight for your dreams – not give up. At last, I was hearing it from the horse's mouth.

'…but only up to a point,' he continued.

'Hmm,' I said vaguely, not yet sure what he was driving at.

'When I lost my old life, I fought for over a year, 24/7, trying to get it back. Put myself through a whole range of different treatments. Can you imagine what that was like?'

I nodded. It sounded all too familiar.

'By the end, I was exhausted and very frustrated. I'd been fighting so hard, I'd even forgotten how to laugh. There was no lightness in my life.'

I nodded again. I was beginning to see where he was headed, but something inside me was resisting.

'I had to stop fighting – to accept that I was never going to realise my old dreams. The sea was my life. Now I can't even swim.' He looked at me. For the first time, his face was serious.

'I see,' I said, but I didn't, not quite. Then I stirred myself. 'But yesterday – you'd never have flown along the beach like that if you hadn't fought, would you?'

'You have to fight to rig up the sail,' Michael said. 'But for the flying itself you need wind.'

I kept nodding; I didn't seem capable of any other response.

'Fighting won't bring my old life back. Fighting won't bring me a good wind. The wind doesn't blow any stronger just because you fight for it or hope for it or wait for it…' He gave me a searching look. In other words, embrace the opportunities that come your way, for they are life's gifts. It probably wasn't too hard for him to guess what I was thinking.

He changed tack. 'Speaking of wind…' He turned, as slowly as a centenarian, to the palms on the other side of Grant Street. Gusts were blowing them back and forth. 'This is a pretty serious topic, but I'm going to leave you now. Let's carry on talking some other time, shall we? Sideshore wind today – great! Must be 19 knots at least, perfect for kite-buggying.' His eyes were shining again; he looked like a child who'd been given a surprise present.

'The coffee's on me,' I said, as he prepared his trike for take-off. His radio had started up with local news from North Queensland.

Michael nodded his thanks. 'Wolf – take care.' That vice-like grip again.

\*    \*    \*

I watched Michael go and was still staring after him long after he'd turned the corner. I wasn't at all happy with what I'd heard, and found myself mulling over the gloomy feeling that sometimes came over me when I was playing with Nina – and her tears in Anzac Park. All that was surely the opposite of Michael's lightness. My talk with him also brought back bad memories of a row I'd had with Anna Amsel before our decision to leave Bonn. Worn out from trying to keep my life on course, despite the storm clouds gathering on the horizon, her words had been as little to my liking as the talk I'd just had with Michael. There were, she said, two ways of finding happiness: either you tried to adapt reality to your dreams – a task that was strenuous and unrewarding – or you took the opposite course and adapted your dreams to fit reality. Had I ever thought about doing that? Happiness researchers had found that the second method led to a great deal more contentment in life. There was, in any case, no such thing as long-term happiness, she said; happiness was like particles of atoms, as elusive as quarks and Higgs bosons. I recall becoming really quite angry. Bloody happiness researchers. I imagined them as people who spent their days studying hemp products in catalogues as they sipped their nettle tea and doled out convoluted advice to the less content. Just like those pseudo-Buddhists who were springing up all over the place, never missing an opportunity to tell you to *let go* of your goals. Hey, you, just let go. *Just let go? Really? Is it that easy? OK, from now on, my greatest dream in life is for an ice lolly.* Ah, that's better, now I'm content. I'll forget all about those other dreams – really *let them go.* Anna Amsel had touched the same sore spot as Michael.

I did realise that our idea of travelling for a million minutes had only taken off once we'd stopped clinging to the notion of an ordinary life in Bonn. In that respect, letting go had been important, but we weren't going to make Nina's difficulties go away by relaxing and lowering our sights. Her fire-brigade dream was a good example. We weren't going to make it happen by sitting around drinking nettle tea while we waited for good luck to arrive.

*  *  *

My coffee had gone cold, so I paid and set off. I needed to pull myself together because we had a busy day ahead of us getting ready for Nina's birthday. There was to be a cake in the afternoon, for which I had abdicated responsibility, pleading lack of talent – but a bonfire was planned for the evening and that was primal enough to tempt me to take charge. Perhaps building a fire on the beach would calm me down. Vera had gently pointed out that fires were strictly forbidden on the beach and that, as non-Aussies, we maybe ought to stick to the rules, so we'd had a family vote and Mr Simon had partaken in his first-ever ballot. As the birthday girl, Nina had three votes, so the result was an overwhelming majority of five to one. Good old democracy. The children helped me gather heaps of wood. Palm fronds burn at least as well as northern European kindling, and fibrous coconut shells make pretty good fuel, too.

At last we were ready, and the party on Four Mile Beach could begin. We lit the fire at dusk. It was beautiful. Sabrina and Lou had come, along with our neighbours and a few other new friends. We played music and prepared delicious food: baked potatoes, fish marinated in thyme and garlic and cooked in foil, baked bananas with honey, the inevitable sausages for the kids and fresh bread. It was bliss. Night settled over Port Douglas like a cloak. First the houses on Solander Boulevard disappeared, then the palms on the beach, and eventually, sitting gathered around the bonfire, we felt as if we were the only people on a small sandy planet, hurtling through space.

Then, suddenly, we were surrounded by bright lights and looming monsters. Parking up at the turning area at the end of the boulevard was one enormous and one smaller fire engine from the local fire station, both with flashing blue lights.

'Step back!' a voice ordered. 'Step back!'

Five men in firefighters' uniforms, three of them in full protective gear, were marching up the beach towards us, visors down and protective shields held in front of them. They looked like the creatures in the *Predator* films. Mr Simon howled, as walkie-talkie voices crackled on all sides and torches flashed in our eyes. Two more firefighters approached, dragging heavy boxes of all kinds of equipment; a roll of hose landed right on my feet. One man had a huge container of extinguishing fluid on his back. It can't have been much fun lugging that around in the tropical evening heat; the thing must have held 40 litres of fluid, and it rarely drops below 25 degrees in Port Douglas at night (plus ten degrees' heat factor from the bonfire). In fact, the whole situation was far from fun.

'This is crazy,' I said to our friends, who nodded with resigned smiles. Nobody said *I told you so.* They moved away from the fire, grabbing our possessions as they went.

I took Nina's arm and led her a few metres away from the blaze, then checked on Vera and Sabrina, who were cuddled up out of harm's way with Mr Simon and Lou, the two babies now crying in unison.

'But why?' said Nina. She was horrified. I could tell she didn't have a clue what was going on. This wasn't at all how she'd imagined her birthday celebration. Another superlative intercultural cock-up – but this time we had only ourselves to blame. Or rather: *I* had only myself to blame, as I had ignored Vera's vote against the fire in favour of the children's wishes, when perhaps they weren't old enough to make an informed decision. It may have been a draconian law in my opinion, but it was the law around here. I felt deeply guilty, but also worried. After all, this was Nina's birthday party. It was *her* bonfire.

The men started pumping foam onto the fire. Scraps of the stuff flew through the air – something else that's wet and falls from the sky, I thought, but this really wasn't the time to say that. Some of the baked potatoes and a few glowing twigs were dislodged and rolled about, spraying sparks onto the sand.

One of the besuited, behelmeted monsters approached us and flipped up his visor. There was a face underneath. 'You can't make a fire here,' he said sharply to me.

Somehow he had known who the ringleader was.

'Oh, can't we? I'm sorry, I didn't know that.'

It can't have been more than a few metres to the nearest of the 20-odd no-bonfire signs dotted along the beach, next to the crocodile and jellyfish warnings. The man was busy unrolling something but stopped abruptly and looked at me, eyebrows raised and lips pursed.

'I'm really sorry,' I said quickly. This wasn't the moment to play dumb.

Luckily, he laughed. 'Nice try, mate,' he said, returning to his roll of hose.

But I hadn't given up; I had to save the fire somehow.

'It's a relatively small fire,' I pointed out.

Surely it was pretty funny that they'd mobilised the entire local fire brigade to put out one humble bonfire? It didn't seem worth the trouble.

He was quick off the mark. 'Good opportunity for a relatively big quarterly drill though,' he said with a grin. 'This'd cost you otherwise.'

Thank God he had a sense of humour.

'I'm really very sorry,' I said, backing down. Then one last attempt. 'It's my daughter's birthday. She asked for the bonfire specially.'

The man stopped unrolling and looked at Nina, who was still stunned by this unexpected turn of events.

'Oh, damn, I see.' There wasn't a hint of sarcasm in his voice. 'Really?' For a six-foot-five monster in Kevlar riot gear, he was surprisingly sensitive.

I nodded.

He thought for a second. 'What's your little girl called?' he asked.

'Nina,' I said.

The man nodded and marched over to the boxes of equipment, rummaged around in one of them and brought out a bright red megaphone. I flinched when he turned it on as it chirped and crackled all down the beach. 'Firewoman Nina, we need your help.'

His amplified voice must have carried all the way to Anzac Park. Two of the other firemen stopped what they were doing to stare at him in astonishment, and he signalled to them not to worry.

Nina looked at me in bewilderment. Her face was already red from all the excitement.

I stammered something incoherent, probably looking as bewildered as she did. I glanced at the fireman again, just to make sure. I'm pretty sure he winked at me, and then he waved Nina over. 'Firewoman Nina, please join us. We urgently need your help.'

'Go on,' I said.

Nina looked uncertain, but less flustered now. She staggered over to the fireman, slowly at first, because she's always wobbly on her feet when she's excited, then more steadily. By the time she reached him, she was smiling all over her face. The man thrust a pair of enormous gloves into her hands, and a red lacquered tool like a big snow shovel. He told her she was the only one who could shovel the fire sand onto the embers – quite a dangerous job. No, not into the wind... Yes, that's the way to do it!

'Thank you, firewoman! We were lucky to find you here.' Nina was shovelling for her life. The handle was almost twice her height and the empty fingers of the gloves stuck out every which way. 'Great job!'

If it had been up to her, she'd have carried on until the entire Four Mile Beach had been shovelled onto that square metre of bonfire.

\* \* \*

I had to carry Nina for the last stretch of the walk home and she fell asleep in my arms. She felt so light. I couldn't remember when she'd last done that, but it seemed fitting that nothing should come between the fire-brigade party and sleep. When I laid her on her bed, a smile flickered across her face. From her clothes, little heaps of sand trickled out and were deposited in the folds of her bedding. The resin from the branches we'd gathered for the fire was dark and sticky in her palms. Her fair hair was all over the place, and a few strands clung to her temples. Her T-shirt had attracted flakes of ash. She sighed softly in her sleep. I covered her with the duvet and switched off the light. At the door, I turned one last time. Who knew what she'd dream about that night?

'Good luck!' I whispered into the darkness. The curtains at the window billowed gently in the wind. As I left her room, I smiled. There it was: the wind, the good luck that Michael patiently waited for so that his kite buggy would fly across the beach.

Later that evening I scrolled through my journal, looking for the page where I had written how important it was to fight for our dreams; that if you want to learn how to sail, you have to set sail. I added: *but you cannot make the wind blow. That's a gift...*

# PEACE AND FREEDOM
# AND ALL THAT

630,000TH MINUTE
WALLABY CREEK FESTIVAL
CAPE YORK PENINSULA (15°45'S, 145°16'E)
QUEENSLAND, AUSTRALIA

'TOURISTS – OUGHT TO PITY THEM REALLY! COOPED up in offices all their lives, sticking to the fucking rules, and then they go and buy some pathetic mini-freedom package from a travel agency, take themselves off on a mini-break somewhere and feel like the bee's fucking knees. Until, whoops, it's back to suburbia and life in a golden cage, y'know?'

'Yeah.'

'So fucking middle class, y'know? That's not real freedom, man. That's fuck all. Totally suburban, know what I mean?'

'Yeah, man.'

'And anal too… They're so unfree, they're even monogamous. Man, I'm telling you. Completely unfree. Morx said the same.'

'Totally unfree.'

'Guy can't even smoke a pipe properly.'

'Yeah, man. Got any of that gear left?'

The first voice was indisputably that of Phoenix, one of the uncrowned but self-assured elders of Queensland's travelling hippy community, so it was fair to assume that the second voice belonged to his young disciple Rainbow, though it was hard to be certain, because I'd barely heard Rainbow say a word when we'd been sitting around the campfire. He was a quiet type, at least when Phoenix was holding forth, which was pretty much all the time. There could be no doubt though, that whether I liked it or not, the man they had declared the most anally retentive suburbanite of the century was me. It was about an hour ago that I'd committed the faux pas with the pipe. How was I supposed to intuitively know the correct method of smoking what Phoenix had informed me was a 'real Navajo peace pipe', without singeing those real black eagle feathers? It sounded as if the mellow gathering at the bonfire would remember me not only for the pungent smell of burnt wing, but also for the damage I'd done to their positive vibes. I'd sneaked away when the discussion on free love had begun to heat up: Mr Simon had needed changing and I'd seized my chance. But here we were, an hour later, only a few metres from each other on either side of a hedge. The nearest festival Portaloo had been rendered off-limits by a large, bad-tempered huntsman spider, so the hedge was serving as a temporary gents'. And without meaning to, I had just eavesdropped on their verdict.

It was pretty damning, but it had its funny side. There was an irony to being condemned as an anally retentive suburbanite on a mini-break when I had been repeatedly labelled a dropout by my friends and colleagues in Bonn.

*   *   *

By this time we had reached Cape York, the northernmost tip of Australia. The world we had dropped out of – our *golden cage*, as Phoenix had called it – was thousands of kilometres away, many more than the earth's diameter; and in terms of adventure and culture shock, the worlds we were dropping into felt even further away than that – more like a distant genuine parallel universe.

By now we'd been away for over 14 months, long enough to have left behind not only a place but also a set of time structures, a whole pattern of living.

Our daily routine began to change after only about six weeks. We thought nothing of letting the children sleep as long as they liked in the mornings and stay up late in the evenings, later than we would have dared admit to our non-dropout friends back in Germany. In fact, our sense of time was gradually slipping away from us altogether: we no longer had appointments to keep; we never had any reason to rush. *No stresstic!*

I soon lost my ability to guess the time with any accuracy. Not wearing a watch (or wearing a non-watch, as I chose to view it) was an essential part of my metamorphosis. I wondered who was wearing my Piaget now – maybe a man who did not have much time. Roughly two months into our trip, I lost my grip on the days of the week. There was no longer any difference between a Friday and a Sunday. We had no work to do; every day was a day off and the sun was always shining. By the time we'd been gone nine months, we were even decidedly hazy about dates. 'What's the date today?' I'd ask Vera. 'I think it's still November,' she would guess. We'd got used to drifting in time like a rudderless ship on the open sea.

But now we had a new golden cage, a rattling blue 1996 Ford Falcon that we called Falco, a vast ship of an estate car with the most environmentally unfriendly engine imaginable. We had bought Falco in Port Douglas to make trips to the surrounding Tablelands, Daintree National Park and the coast around Cape Tribulation. Cars like that are very popular down under; the locals load them with sheep or bricks until the back tyres begin to bulge outwards, and young tourist couples black out the back windows and stretch out to sleep in the boot in public car parks to avoid paying $65 a night in the east coast campsites. Demand has driven up the price of second-hand Falcons, and trafficking the cars is a job in its own right; whole flotillas of them are regularly driven down the east coast to be sold in the south to buyers who set off again on the long trek north. We bought ours for a mere $2,800 and thought it a bargain, until our friend Will sheepishly pointed out the strange rust marks on the interior metalwork. He was right, of course – the cigar lighter had rusted to pieces, the hinge of the glove compartment was a dark flaky red and the rails under the front seats looked as if they'd been stolen from a Bronze Age tomb. Every true Queenslander knows what that means: the car must have been parked in one of those coveted parking spaces on the promenade during the latest cyclone. But Will didn't want to be gloomy, and assured us that it generally took a while for the salt to eat its way into the electronics. He did admit, though, that there was no halting the destruction process.

We just hoped there hadn't been any sheep or sleeping tourists in the boot when the car was flooded, and cheerfully drove our economic loss back and forth across North Queensland. A generous application of superglue did its bit to prolong Falco's life.

For the ultimate in suburban luxury, we supplemented our car with a half-open tent and self-inflating sleeping mats and set off for the Wallaby Creek Festival, a family-friendly hippy music festival in the rainforest. Our second-hand sleeping mats were another misjudged bargain: we realised when we tried to blow them up that the valve caps were missing. The mats were only about half a metre across and had the consistency of damp cardboard. I took it in turns to share mine with a bigger child who had no intention of sleeping and a smaller child who very much wanted to sleep but couldn't. The question of whether *I* was bothered by the stones and roots didn't arise. Perhaps I should have noted in my journal that sometimes it really is OK to buy new kit, but as this didn't fit well with our downsizing euphoria, I decided to be cleverer next time.

\* \* \*

The festival was in full swing when we arrived, and our little idyll was surrounded by hundreds of other tents and even more VW camper vans in faded rainbow colours. It was, I decided, something like the manager seminar on Ko Phra Thong, only without the managers and without any seminars. Many of the people here were professional hippies, having evidently skipped the CEO phase and headed straight for dropout-dom.

It was a laid-back affair. The spectrum of occupations at the festival ranged from professional slackliners, acrobats, magicians, jugglers and obstacle-course runners to musicians and drummers to wood-carvers, instrument-makers and driftwood-sellers – one of the alternative career options I had listed in my journal: it was already a certified profession! All these people were serious and passionate about their enthusiasms, but only when they felt like it. Many of them were also extremely enterprising; the place was littered with buskers' hats to catch coins in. Almost nothing on display had any recognisable use to me; dreamcatchers, incense burners, jewellery made from everyday objects... nothing electronic. Whether woven, carved, moulded or painted, almost everything was handmade. My favourite was a chocolate stall run by a hippie woman called Rosalynd, who had bought up what looked like every chocolate casualty from every factory in Australia. She toured the festivals with her hundreds of kilos of smashed chocolate and sold it on, at a considerable profit.

Nina and Mr Simon adored Rosalynd, who plied them with chocolate, not minding that their little pockets were full of sticks and stones rather than money. (I added *broken chocolate-dealer* to the list of potential jobs in my journal.) The best event of the festival from the children's point of view was a ceremony performed by a group of Aboriginal Australians. It was a dance that depicted a dreamtime journey to their ancestors, and was sensational enough for Nina to decide that festivals were among the best things on earth. While we were watching them dance, she held her breath and squeezed my hand with excitement. It was Nina who suggested that, if I were to take up a proper profession again, I should become an *Arborichie*. In the days that followed, she was completely committed to establishing their dance as our own family ritual. I could only manage the rhythmic, half-squat movements for 30 seconds and was told to practise harder. To Vera's great amusement, Nina and I spent quite some time seriously training together.

Considering that this was the first alternative music festival of my life, I thought I coped pretty well at Wallaby Creek. I had spent a deprived childhood in the costume stores and prompter's box of the Düsseldorf Opera House on the Rhine, brought up by parents who regarded festivals without Mozart as something for dropouts – though, of course, Mozart himself was seen as something of a punk by his contemporaries.

Phoenix was right to recognise that I was not a follower of counterculture. My hair, thank God, was too short even for the most basic of dreadlocks. I was no good at any kind of arts and crafts and couldn't even weave a decent dreamcatcher. And for most of my adult life, I had pursued a professional career with a matching income and a sensible pension. As far as Phoenix was concerned, I might as well have sold my soul to old Mephisto.

Nevertheless, there was always the question of personal freedom to consider. And to hippies like Phoenix and Rainbow, that was non-negotiable, for dropouts and suburbanites alike.

* * *

I had been introduced to Phoenix's revolutionary understanding of freedom during our last evening at the festival.

When the big stages went quiet, small groups formed all over the festival grounds, gathered around bonfires and musicians. Bonfires had always held a magnetic attraction for Nina, even before her firefighting operation. She made a beeline for a group of hippies lolling around a veggie barbecue. Among them, an extremely good-looking man was playing his grandparents' favourites on a guitar with a certain virtuosity: the Stones, the Eagles, Cat Stevens, Jimi Hendrix. More important for Nina, Rosalynd (or *Rosalyndi*, as Nina called her) was one of the group. The question of where we would spend our last evening was settled.

It seemed, however, that you needed Phoenix's approval before being accepted into this flock. There could be no doubt that he was the alpha male of the group, and the others – all female or of uncertain gender, except for the guitarist – were mere disciples. Phoenix resembled Charlton Heston as Moses in *The Ten Commandments* and looked at least as old. He wore flowing white robes, brown Jesus sandals, huge chunks of lapis lazuli on his hands and around his neck, sported a grey-white beard that extended down to his navel and held a stick with a spiral carved into the wood below the handle. This bombastic kitsch was finished off with a blue bandana around his head.

Nina adored Phoenix as soon as she set eyes on him. She regarded him as a natural authority. It was partly down to his lovely way of expressing himself.

'Greetings, noble friend. Approach and bestow on us the light of your presence.'

Those were the first words he spoke to me.

'It's nice to meet you too,' I said.

He seemed to have a severe squint, as his eyes were all over the place. I followed his gaze and found myself staring at Vera's breasts. The guy had taste. And despite his venerable age, he was evidently still quite the ladies' man.

Good on you, Moses, I thought.

'And who do we have here?' he asked, turning to Vera and wrapping his arms around her in a rather one-sided embrace; she didn't have much choice in the matter. His long white beard stuck into the air at an angle and his white robes fluttered in the wind.

'I'm Nina,' said Nina, before Vera could say anything, and proceeded to wrap *her* arms around one of Vera's legs and Phoenix's billowing white robes. Nina can be overly familiar with strangers, but her instinct doesn't often fail her. A man who speaks like a drunk medieval lord – and what's more, looks like one, too – has to be a good person.

While the womenfolk were still entangled with Phoenix, Mr Simon had toddled over to the barbecue and was standing in front of the red-hot veggies, his eyes shining. I hurried to intervene before the inevitable attempted food theft. Did the hungry and inexperienced Mr Simon realise that what he was ogling was not grilled chicken? Those vegetarians don't have it easy, I considered, looking at the barbecued aubergines covered in melted cheese; meat-eaters despise them for being sectarian and vegans deplore their half-heartedness.

The assembled *hippies*, as Nina had called them, draped over cool boxes, beer crates and blankets, smiled a hello at us. It was time for the true-to-form hippie introductions.

'Behold our friend Vera!' announced Phoenix. 'And her young companion.' That was me. Phoenix had at last released Vera and now stood, his arms thrust heavenwards, as if he were about to proclaim the Ten Commandments.

I glanced at Vera, who smiled back. All was well. She could take care of herself.

'Please honour us with your esteemed presence. We must make time for deep friendship in this brief existence of ours.' Phoenix looked at Vera and patted the space next to him.

'And I'm Nina,' said Nina, introducing herself again. This was astonishing, as she was usually far more timid. She knelt down on the spot Phoenix had offered to Vera and took the hem of his robes in her hands. 'You have a very nice dress,' she said, stroking the cloth admiringly. Vera sat down next to her, grinning.

'What peace there is in the air,' said Phoenix, staring knowingly into the distance. I would have called it a strong smell of hash, but Phoenix seemed to like speaking in metaphors. The good-looking young man, whose far-sighted parents had named him Rainbow some 19 years previously, was fiddling around, trying to light an oversized pipe hung with black feathers. Rainbow inhaled and had a coughing fit, knocking over a bottle of beer, the contents of which seeped into the parched grass. It must have been months since it had rained.

'So sorry,' said Rainbow, looking almost subserviently at Phoenix, who forgave him with a generous wave of his hand.

The pipe made the rounds. When it got to me, I somehow contrived to let it overheat so that one of the feathers began to smoke, and swiftly passed it on to the next disciples along, whose names sounded like Aniston and Harmony. At this stage, nobody appeared to have noticed my error. Eventually, a very young woman who could have been Phoenix's granddaughter and had introduced herself with a big smile as 'Shanti from Vienna', passed it on to Phoenix. He thanked her with a lingering kiss on the mouth, but didn't for a second take his eyes off the rest of his flock; like a lion, permanently on his guard.

Phoenix turned out to be a good friend of *Morx* and *Angels*, as he pronounced their names. Karl Marx, in particular, shared his opinions on practically everything, from the quality of the weed that was being consumed here in such large quantities to the matter of free love. Clearly Phoenix had no trouble finding an audience for his stories. Indeed, he was probably Cape York's first self-styled apostle of historical and dialectical materialism and Marxist free love. As far as I could remember, Marx married his childhood sweetheart and had seven children. Hadn't the wealthier Engels saved the Marx ménage from the tribulations of free love by claiming fatherhood of a child Marx had sired with his house-keeper in the broom cupboard? Who knows what would have become of the communist project if he hadn't stepped in? With an extra mouth to feed, Marx might have abandoned his writing and gone to work in a factory. But I kept my remarks to myself – they would have been out of place in the chilled atmosphere of that peaceful, balmy summer's night.

One crucial insight of *Morx*, Phoenix told us, was that a partnership between only *two* people – he stressed the word *two* as if it were the punchline of a joke – was a purely capitalist affair. Somehow contriving to wink encouragingly at Vera while at the same time giving Shanti a lingering pat, he explained that for centuries men had used marriage as a smokescreen to treat women as their property and oppress them. That was *Morx*'s big discovery, and his answer was to set up the world's first holistic commune in Brussels with *Angels* – a place where love was a gift freely and regularly given, according to Phoenix. Rainbow hung on Phoenix's words, nodding his approval. He looked, I thought, not only as beautiful as Snow White but as naive, with all that peace circulating around his lungs.

Since then, Phoenix told us, lack of freedom had been a thing of the past. (Conspiratorial winking at Vera, followed by a shifty glance at me.) Rainbow strummed his guitar. Harmony and Shanti-from-Vienna sang along softly to 'Hotel California'.

'Of course, first you have to strip yourself down,' Phoenix went on, chewing his barbecued aubergine. I had a feeling this wasn't a metaphor. He probably regarded stripping as an important step on the road to mental freedom. 'Freedom is the will to cast off social conventions,' he added. 'Like a T-shirt you no longer need.'

*I knew it.*

Rosalynd took the tension out of the situation by fetching a big box of chocolate from her car and handing it around. She didn't seem overly interested in Phoenix's ideology. I wasn't even sure she was a Phoenix disciple, though she certainly blended in with the rest of the flock as far as her appearance went.

Rainbow coughed again after a particularly deep drag on the pipe, and mustering all his courage declared, 'Freedom's when you've nothing left to lose.' Little puffs of smoke came out of his mouth as he spoke.

Shanti, too, had something to share with us: freedom was being able to do what you wanted, wasn't it? It was simple. Harmony nodded enthusiastically.

'And what does freedom mean to our young friend here?' Phoenix asked challengingly, pointing at me with a lapis-lazuli-laden hand.

'It seems to me that freedom is something very subjective this evening,' Vera put in, with a mollifying look in my direction.

'Anyone else for chocolate?' Rosalynd asked quickly.

The question of freedom was tricky, I thought to myself. How can there be one freedom that applies to everybody? To Curitiba Man and Cro-Magnon Man? To Marxists and entrepreneurs, hippie extremists and Passat Comfortline drivers, building-society savers and inveterate globetrotters? Each to his own? That didn't quite work, but the subject was worth discussing. It was a pity that it had been abused to promote free love à la Phoenix that evening, and that half the people who might have contributed to the discussion were already stoned.

'Maybe freedom is being able to spend your evenings by a bonfire eating chocolate,' I mumbled. It was a peace offering to Phoenix, but it fell on stony ground.

'*Morx* wouldn't see it like that,' he began, jabbing the air with his finger. He was apparently capable of conducting a dialogue even without a proper interlocutor.

'From *Morx*'s point of view…' he went on.

I couldn't stop myself. 'Tolstoy here,' I said, my temper finally triggered, 'has to go and free his son from his shitty nappy.'

My reference to the great Russian writer and aristocrat (who was also a pacifist and a liberal) fell like a bomb. Phoenix threw me a look of disapproval, Vera giggled, Harmony choked on her aubergine and Rainbow choked on his pipe smoke. I grabbed a protesting Mr Simon.

'I don't want to go to bed,' Nina shrieked into the silence a fraction of a second later. That, too, was a kind of freedom: staying up as long as you like.

'Another five minutes,' Vera said, nodding at her and smiling pacifyingly at me. 'I'll just gather up our things, OK?'

'Great, I'll go on ahead,' I said, and trudged off to the tent with an angry Mr Simon. We had a long, mosquito-filled night ahead of us, and so it was that after an hour's tossing and turning I found myself at the hedge, inadvertently eavesdropping on Phoenix and Rainbow.

\*   \*   \*

As we hurtled over the dusty surface of Mulligan Highway towards Port Douglas the next morning, so we'd be back in time for Sabrina's birthday party, Nina suddenly produced a red packet tied with blue hemp string from a tissue.

'I have a big secret here,' she said proudly. 'Rosalyndi told me to give you this.'

She must have been hoarding the packet like a treasure all morning. No one had noticed it when we'd loaded the car. Now that I thought about it, she had been unusually quiet.

When I opened it, I found four enormous bars of chunky, slightly melted milk chocolate with macadamia nuts. My favourite.

'That's nice of her, isn't it?' Nina said, thrilled.

Then I spotted a little slip of red paper. I unfolded it. In ornate letters, it said:

*Freedom is always the freedom of dissenters* ☺
*Love, Rosa.*

# MUD. BRICK. HOME

690,002ND MINUTE
RUBY'S COTTAGE
ROSEWOOD BAY (a secret place on the Great Southern Ocean)
WESTERN AUSTRALIA

- 50—75 big spadefuls of earth
- 25 drops of sweat
- ½ a 20kg sack of cement
- 30 minutes
- 2 flasks of tea
- I big bucket of water, nice and full
- blood
- sun

BETWEEN AUGUSTA AND ESPERANCE, THE SOUTHERN
coast of the state of Western Australia is relatively undeveloped,
at least from the perspective of a central European infrastructural
planner. Western Australia has the longest coastline in the country
and the people who live on its western side have to travel a good
1,500km to get to the north, but the inhabitants of WA have mainly
chosen to settle in a narrow band around the bottom, perhaps
because it is so beautiful there. On Google Earth, it looks as if an
enormous wave came along one morning and washed a heap of
model houses, toy cars and miniature streets onto one corner of
a giant island to form Walpole, Peaceful Bay, Rosewood Bay and
Albany. Between settlements stretch miles of unpopulated beaches,

many of them national parks. If you sail along the coast at night, you can go for hours without seeing a light. Land and night seem to merge into overwhelming loneliness, while what Australians call the Great Southern Ocean – a suitably reverential name for such an awe-inspiring body of water – crashes, unrestrained and wild, onto steep cliffs in a hissing, spitting liquid firework display. This is a rocky coast of several hundred kilometres, interspersed with beaches. The spray from the surf flies so high that it makes rainbows; the ground roars, and no one ventures closer than 20 metres from the cliff edge.

A month and a half after the festival, we started renting a small cottage in the centre of Rosewood Bay, about 100 metres from the only set of traffic lights in the village. The owner had inherited it when his grandmother died in 2009 and it looked as if nothing had been changed since the 1960s, but there was a garden. The sky was stunning in those summer months – the whole world seemed drenched in brightness. In the mornings, I had only to open the heavy curtains a crack and a ray of sun would slice through the dark room, while outside, iridescent flecks of light danced on the silver leaves of the trees like myriad little mirrors, as if the sky were hung with disco balls. Even when it clouded over, we needed sunglasses to stop our faces aching from the strain of screwing up our eyes.

Rosewood Bay, a former lumberjack settlement, is situated on the river of the same name. On the edge of the village, the Rosewood River flows into a huge inlet, an ocean bay that, for part of the year, is separated from the open sea by natural sandbanks. It's a long time since there were any lumberjacks here, and these days, the gnarled paperbark trees growing on the riverbanks outnumber the people.

Life here is homespun, simple and often lived barefoot. In this patient but powerful landscape, the people live quiet lives. In the evenings, they sit at their rough-hewn kitchen tables in their creaking cottages; here and there, a glimmer of light shows in a window, and you can see locals playing cards or agonising over how to finance a much-needed new water tank, or what to plant in their vegetable patches.

The concept of earthiness is important in Rosewood Bay. Houses, for instance. The more crooked, makeshift, do-it-yourself and witchy a house is, the higher it rises on the scale, and the very earthiest of all lie nestled in the fairy-tale woods, like hobbit caves in The Shire. A brightly painted bike can pass for earthy, too, if it has a basket decorated with flowers and knitted handlebar-warmers – and an earthy party is one with leathery barbecued apples instead of chips, fiddles instead of techno and cinnamon instead of cocaine. (The way I saw it, the earthy people of Rosewood Bay were pretty much the exact opposite of Western Australia's self-appointed upper class, the cokehead hipsters of South Perth.)

Another earthy aspect of village life was bartering. One neighbour might have a whole heap of tomatoes at the back of his shed, while another had just caught his first pollock (a vast fish, too big for one family). Somebody had freshly made grape must to barter, and someone else had just felled a tree and had stacks of best red jarrah, wood so hard you'd think the axe was connecting with steel. Jars of pickled squash were exchanged for a leg of kangaroo. Anything that was no longer wanted was deposited on a street corner in the early mornings – half a crate of this, a few buckets of that, an old bike. You paid by pushing your dollar notes under a length of wire wrapped around a tree, and I don't think anyone knew where the damp, limp notes went. Sometimes the nouveau riche left their yachts there in the hope of selling them, but they tended to end up growing moss. More useful were the unmanned fruit and veg stalls scattered about the place, with honesty tin cans to put your money in. Nina thought this *rather risky* and was afraid that nasty robbers might come along and take all the lovely mangos.

Hugging trees was pretty earthy, and the women in particular, seemed able to indulge without anyone batting an eyelid. Sometimes the people of Rosewood Bay staged woodland plays featuring talking leaves. 'Logical,' said Nina, nodding, the first time we watched one. Then there was the Red Tent for women only, where participants met every month to share their experiences, along with fortifying vegetable soup.

The Rosewoodian philosophy of life was right up our street, not least because we had arrived there with Little Miss Earthy herself. Nina's *inside-out puddle trick*, for example – a stunt that involved transferring almost the entire contents of a puddle into her wellington boots with a few strategically aimed jumps – won her the instant approval of the kids next door. The portable terrariums in her jacket pockets, too, were soon famous. Soon every child in the neighbourhood knew that Nina could be relied on to provide refuge for lonely earthworms from the playground (in her left pocket) or woodlice from the car park outside our favourite local café (in her right pocket, which had a zip). Nina was quite the expert in relation to all small creatures. She knew where the most poisonous spiders lived and where the birds' nests were, and she and Mr Simon kept a whole host of extremely earthy finds under the veranda, which Vera and I weren't supposed to know about. Soon Nina had made even more friends at the playground, where there was always someone around to play with because some intelligent person had built the public gas barbecues next door.

One day, someone knocked to offer us tomato seeds and shrivelled seed potatoes, and when that happened, we knew we had become true (if partial and temporary) residents of Rosewood. Not long afterwards we had our first invitations to barbecues in the park and were asked if we'd like to help make waffles on Busy Bees Day at the local woodland school.

It's a small village, so a lot of the cultural ways of thinking were completely new to us. One of these was the link between the land and the people. I sensed a whole mesh of connections in Rosewood Bay, but as a newcomer I couldn't quite pin them down. Somehow, everything and everyone seemed to be intertwined, as if people were rooted not only in the land, but also in each other. The Rosewoodians were always talking about *their land* and what they were doing with it. The topic was so ubiquitous that I sometimes had the impression that the whole of Western Australia was one big plot of land that the proud Aussies had divvied up between them. Whenever I met anyone – especially men – I often felt, in spite of their warm welcome, that I was being kept at a distance; I felt acutely aware that I was on somebody else's land, not on anonymous no-man's-land where anyone could come and go. It was in Western Australia that I first had the sense that humans act territorially.

If city dwellers have territory of their own, it begins at their front door. In Rosewood Bay, it begins as soon as you turn off the road onto their narrow, bumpy drive; as soon as you pass the crooked mailbox thick with red dust – a kind of signpost that announces you are entering new territory. A family's land is a concrete expression of the abstract notion of family. Land quietly outlives the curious twists and turns of an individual's life. Although we made a lot of friends in Rosewood, I felt sure that any outsider would never be anything but a guest until the day he drove a stake into land of his own.

I often found myself pondering the matter of the land and its people, and one day I asked Joe about it. He and his wife had recently bought some land and begun to build a house.

'Land's pretty important here, isn't it?' I asked.

'How do you mean?'

'Not sure of that myself,' I said, grinning. 'I've just noticed that it matters to you. Where we come from in Germany – in the cities, at least – hardly anyone talks about *land*. We have savings accounts and terraced houses and back gardens, but *land* as such doesn't mean much to us.'

Joe just nodded.

'Here in Rosewood Bay, the land seems to connect you, as if there's a network of roots linking you together. What do you think?'

'Hmm,' said Joe. 'There might be something in that.'

'Do you think we could meet for a coffee sometime?' I asked. 'You could tell me a bit about it.'

Joe thought for a while. Then he asked, 'Got any plans for Tuesday? I'd like to show you something.'

I had no plans for Tuesday. I had no plans for Monday or Wednesday either, come to that. I always had time to spare, and if I found something I wanted to do, I could just do it. That was the beauty of our million-minute life.

These were the ingredients:

1. Sleeping in as long as we wanted.

2. Thinking about what we would love to do.

3. Doing what we loved to do.

4. Recovering from doing what we loved to do.

5. Staying up as late as we wanted.

Variations were doing the same thing with our new friends, plus picnic or a barbecue. Another alternative was not to think about what to do, and then do nothing at all – just float through the day. Super-sensational things would happen anyway; for example:

- A blue snail trying to commit suicide in the chimney.

- Jumping the biggest wave ever.

- Our car breaking down in the middle of nowhere (again).

- Harvesting green tomatoes before they were ripe from our own veggie patch, a joy for apparently colour-blind kids.

- Trying to laugh louder than the kookaburras who perched on trees and telegraph poles (no mean feat).

- Nina teaching us *Aborichie* dances, and spending a lot of time creating *didgledeedoos* from literally every material that came in the form of a pipe.

- Building dams (even where it was forbidden).

- Finding a harpoon or a bow or a fishing rod or a submarine in the garden that was pretending to be an ordinary branch.

- Finding a real whalebone as tall as me during a beachcombing expedition, and adding it to the 1.7 tonnes of shells that we had transported individually into our garden.

During these beautiful days, we explored and reinterpreted what felt like a whole planet of adventure in slow motion and in microscopic detail, with endless laughter. Even I had completely recovered from MAID. Not a single minute was ever declared to be boring – it was as if the word didn't exist.

\*    \*    \*

'Can I bring Nina?' I asked Joe.

'Sure,' he said, 'as long as she's happy to watch. You'll also need sturdy shoes, work clothes and a flask of tea.'

We met at seven in the morning on a plot of land that belonged to Joe's parents. Joe took us to the far end, where some of the earth had been removed and construction equipment was standing around.

'What do you see here?' Joe pointed to the spot I was standing on.

I looked down at my shoes. Soil – very sandy soil; the sea must have been here once. And a few stones. I lifted a foot to make sure I hadn't missed anything. My soles had left a chequered pattern in the soil.

'A heap of earth?' I ventured.

'Exactly,' said Joe with satisfaction, as if I'd solved a riddle. 'Earth. Land.' He pushed some of it into a small pile with his shoe. 'This is the land of my fathers. Let's get going.'

He gave me very precise instructions, then poured petrol into a compressor from a green canister and switched the machine on. It started up noisily. A tube from the compressor led to a cement mixer, a heavy steel monster whose cement-coated drum now ground into motion.

Joe thrust a spade into my hand and searched for the spot where I'd been standing. 'Watch carefully,' he said, and drove his spade as deep as he could into the sandy earth, through my chequered footprint. On a good spade, the head is 'treaded' on the top to prevent you from ruining your shoes on the sharp metal edge. The first spadefuls landed in the mixer drum with a dull *clong*, like a cracked bell. After that, earth fell on earth and was hardly audible above the noise of the compressor, except when a stone rattled against the inside of the drum now and then.

'Just 35 spadefuls to be going on with.'

He let me get on with it. I was soon out of breath.

'Before you add the cement, you have to pour in water, so it doesn't make too much dust... Like this.' The water from the stained yellow bucket vanished into the drum. Then Joe lugged a 20kg sack of cement over from the shed and rammed a trowel into the thick paper. Half the sack was enough for one load. He was right about the dust: a thin film of cement settled on the sweaty skin of my lower arms and crunched between my teeth – finer than sand on the beach, almost like chewing toothpaste. I liked the smell of wet cement – it reminded me of sneaking onto building sites in the rain as a child and creeping furtively around the rusty iron rods that supported the building's grey shell. The mixture had to be 15% cement, or it wouldn't hold. Apart from the cement, which he had to buy, Joe needed only one thing: the land he owned.

While the cement mixer was droning away, he showed me a heavy mould of riveted steel plate in the shed. Inside, it was divided into five rows of five individual oblong brick moulds, surrounded by a frame. Altogether, the thing was two metres long and 1.5 metres wide. The moulds had no base, so I could see the plastic sheet that Joe had used to cover the shed floor. In some places, the metal had been scoured bright and smooth. Joe carefully sprayed the moulds with oil, to prevent too much of the mixture sticking to the edges later.

The next step was making sure that the 'dough' – the soil and cement mixture – was the right consistency. Joe was absolutely focused: if the mixture ends up too runny (perhaps because you fail to take into account that the earth is still wet after a downpour the night before) it can take ages to harden, wobbling around in the mould for hours and slowing down the entire process. If, on the other hand, it turns out too hard (maybe because you spilt too much water from the buckets) there's a risk that some of it will stick to the mould when you pull it out. It isn't like making sand pies, where you can bang the mould down on the sand; you have to use a pulley to extract the contents very gently, so you must be able to depend on your mixture.

Another ten spadefuls. And another ten. By now I had splashes of hardened cement on my face and in my hair, like barnacles sticking to a rock. Nina was riveted by the whole process, and so proud of me. Later that day we made several mini-praline mudbricks. One of my fingernails had bent backwards, and on my right middle finger, the skin was torn above the knuckle. I thought of Curitiba Man. He'd never had any reason to bleed, safely packaged in his sterile bespoke suits like bubble wrap; and the more successful he'd been, the more untouched by DIY he had become.

Since travelling with the children, all that had changed radically. I was more open and more vulnerable, physically as well as mentally and emotionally. Children are always running into things and banging their chins or heads, falling over and grazing knees or elbows or hands, getting their fingers burnt or trapped, cutting them on knives or scissors. Now I was the same, always in the wars. My wound was throbbing. You soon injure yourself when you stop thinking about things and actually do them. I had a huge weeping blister on my left palm that had left a stain on the shaft of the spade.

Joe signalled that the mixture was ready. 'Excellent,' he said.

We tipped the drum of the cement mixer, and the mix slid into a wheelbarrow the size of a huge digger shovel. I tried to push it over to the mould on my own but my body tensed up, while the monster barrow rocked forwards a few centimetres and then rolled back into the ruts left by its two bulging motocross tyres, pushing me with it. With Joe's help, it was doable.

In my Curitiba high-flyer days, I had always thought of myself as a *doer*. I had raced through to-do lists, firing off articles and information from all cylinders. And yet the results had remained intangible: I'd produced nothing but paper. I'd had this notion that scientific findings led to decisions, and decisions to palpable results: a new national park, a new research centre, three hectares of rainforest saved from the chainsaws, money for a new rangers' jeep or workshops for the locals. But the only thing all that paperwork had produced was a lot of hot air. At times I had even felt removed from life – uprooted and bloodless. What had we doers actually done? What had we made? Nothing to compare to this earthy cement mixture that was clinging to my hair right now.

'You all right?' Joe asked, observing me just standing and thinking with a spade in my hand. 'What are you doing?'

'I'm fine,' I said and returned to my shovelling, happy to get on with the job.

We'd come to the best bit, in Nina's and my opinion: the thick sludge had to be divided equally between the moulds with the spade. Sometimes there was a horrible screech of metal scraping against metal when the spade was caught by a rivet in the steel, delivering a painful blow to the wrists. Each individual mould, 35cm long, 20cm broad and 20cm high, had to be carefully filled. If air bubbles formed, the bricks would be weak and friable, so we jabbed our spades frantically through the mix. Now I was really beginning to sweat. Sweat was running down my nose and from my armpits and along the backs of my arms in milky drops, clinging briefly to my elbows before falling and mingling with the earth.

Joe stopped poking about for a moment and broke his silence. He motioned with his glove to a drop of sweat on my nose.

'What we're doing is putting down roots here today,' he said.

Then came the moment of magic – the transformation. Very

carefully, Joe pulled at the rope, where the mould was hanging over a pulley. At first, nothing happened, but then the rope grew tauter and tauter, the truss crunched and gradually the steel began to slide up off the mixture with a juicy smacking sound. It was like watching a child lift a mould off a sandcastle to admire his handiwork. Similarly solemn, too.

There they were.

'So, what do you see now?' Joe asked excitedly, manoeuvring the heavy, dangling moulds out of the way.

'Bricks,' I said. 'Beautiful bricks.' And I meant it. They really were beauties.

'Our *muchbricks*!' said Nina.

They had smooth, plumb edges, and lay in ordered regularity on the spot where only moments before we had tipped a huge heap of sludge into the mould. There were 25 of them, in neat rows. And best of all, they were home-made, not bought. Made from the ground I was standing on. By the sweat of my brow. I would have to add *brick-making* to that list of *really nice things* in the journal I had started on Ko Phra Thong.

'That's right!' Joe grinned at Nina. 'Mud bricks.'

He banged the earth from his trousers. 'Now we can load yesterday's bricks. We haven't had our talk yet,' he said with a smile.

I followed him to the back of the shed where another 25 bricks were waiting, these ones no longer wet and grey but ochre-coloured. That meant that they were half-dry; depending on the weather, mud bricks have to dry for at least 16 hours before they can be stacked and transported. It's another few days before they can be used for building.

We carefully loaded the wooden crates of bricks onto the back of Joe's Toyota Hilux. By the time we were finished, I had an aching back, an aching neck and aching biceps – I felt terrific. We jolted over Joe's plot of land in his ute. The house was already beginning to take shape.

Several hundred mud bricks formed a kind of ground plan. A few of the walls were waist-high; at the back, there were even some that were full height. It takes several thousand bricks to build a house.

'Well?' Joe asked.

'Your home,' I said.

'Our mud-brick home.' He nodded proudly. 'And this is only a tiny part of what you might call the *network of roots*. This room here I built with a friend – the machines are his, too. He and his family are building back there. They've got lovely kids. Maybe they'll play with ours one day, there, in that playroom we'll build on the left. Next week, your bricks will go on that back wall. Your sweat, our earth, our friends… This is where we'll plant veggies.'

As he spoke, Joe pointed to different parts of the plot. His wife had been planting fruit trees already. No matter what kind of storms life threw at them, their home would be their unconditional base. Their children and grandchildren would eat the fruit from their orchard. So the mud bricks, the fruit and the earthy people in Rosewood Bay had something in common – they were, in a quite literal sense, part of this land.

'The wood from that big karri tree will almost see us through the winter,' he continued.

I nodded, transfixed. Life in Rosewood really was all connected.

'How about that coffee?' he asked.

'Let's make another load of bricks first,' I said.

# CHILD'S PLAY

'IT'S POSSIBLE WE CAN MAKE AN EXCEPTION.'

Deep breath. So far, things were looking good. That isn't necessarily to be expected when you turn up out of the blue after nearly a year and a half on the road and ask to register your child in a kindergarten class 'on a trial basis, for about three days a week and probably only a few hours a day'. So far, Nina had been learning about the world through our everyday experiences.

The head of this Steiner school had listened calmly as Vera charmingly pleaded her case, and told us he was sure it would be possible to turn a blind eye to our unorthodox proposal.

'Could you tell us something about this term's learning targets?' I asked.

Vera threw me a furtive annoyed glance. The headmaster's irritation was rather less well concealed.

'Just an outline,' I added, realising it might have been better to avoid the classic helicopter-parent approach. All we wanted, after all, was for Nina to come into contact with other children on a regular basis, like she had at the Port Douglas playgroup where she'd made some lovely friends. Learning targets weren't exactly our top priority. But I was nervous. After our long journey, a kindergarten place was almost exotic, and not something we could take for granted. This would be Nina's first time at an actual school. I also had more personal reasons for my nervousness, but I wasn't going to let on about that.

'Learning targets here tend to be honed to individual needs,' the headmaster said cheerfully. 'Let's wait for your daughter to settle in, then we'll see.'

Vera nodded emphatically and gave me a warning stare. 'Great idea.'

'Sure,' I said.

'A trusting relationship with the parents is, of course, ex-*treme-ly* important to us,' the headmaster said, with a meaningful glance in my direction. 'From the alpha to the omega. I hope we can get to know each other.'

We agreed that Nina would begin by attending for a week. She could start the next day, though it would be a good idea if one of us stayed with her.

We trudged out to the car in near silence, but the floodgates opened almost the moment we turned onto the main road.

'Learning targets?' Vera said. 'Can you give me a quick summary of the learning targets of our trip? Just a sentence. Go on – you can start with the words *Our trip…*'

'So I had a relapse,' I admitted.

'Was that Curitiba Man talking to the headmaster?' she asked.

'More like the Waldorf allergy…'

She looked at me enquiringly. My relations with Steiner (aka Waldorf) schools were rather fraught, but until today I had stashed the memory away. The last time I had set foot in such an establishment – aged four, on my first day at a Waldorf kindergarten – a child undergoing the school's anti-aggression therapy programme had hit me repeatedly over the head with a metal fire engine, while our teacher looked on benevolently, or so it seemed to me. In the end, I'd had to be carried, bleeding, out of the building, and my mother had engaged the services of a childminder called Miss Jessica instead. I reported these historic events to Vera with as much drama as the restricted space in the car would allow.

'Am I right in thinking that this happened some time ago?' Vera asked.

'It was that Atlantis thing too,' I added querulously.

And it was. I'd done a bit of online research into the Steiner curriculum over the last few days and had come across some astonishing material – not least the theory that the human race originated from Atlantis. OK, so I was prepared to accept flying green meercats with blue balls and so on, but this Atlantis story was taking things just a little too far. The world has a plausible evolutionary theory; scientists have studied East African skull fragments, and I'd studied history for a few years. If I'd asked about learning targets, it was because I genuinely wanted to find out whether Nina was going to be taught important stuff like that.

But at least the interview had settled which of us would be accompanying her for her trial week, so the following morning I drove a very excited little girl to her new kindergarten. I ought to mention that this is probably the most beautifully situated school in the world, equalled only, perhaps, by the German International School in Cape Town. The school buildings were erected with loving care on picturesque rolling land; a little river winds its way between copses, vegetable patches, sheep pasture and climbing frames, and everything is bathed in the warm light of the Western Australian sun.

After welcoming a not-too-timid Nina, the school secretary sent her to a beautiful circular playroom with the other children and advised me to take a seat on the playroom sofa until the teacher had a moment to talk to me. I settled down with my journal to jot down a few things I'd been mulling over lately.

I was soon torn from my thoughts by a soft swooshing sound. A cheerful woman swathed entirely in purple came towards me, holding something limp and pink in her hand.

She looked deep into my eyes. 'Yvette,' she said, as graciously as if I were meeting the Queen of England and the Archangel Gabriel rolled into one.

'Wolf. Pleased to meet you.'

Purple Yvette scrutinised me, sitting on the sofa. She took my hand, nodding slowly and saying with a soft, knowing smile, 'Ah, Wolf, the head told me you were coming today. Welcome! It's very important to us to have trusting working relationships with parents.'

Then she opened her hand in slow motion, with a look that said: *here, in my hand, is the solution to all the problems you have failed to solve over the last two decades.* I looked at a bright pink skein; it must have been about half a kilometre of wool.

Gently, she put it down on a table in front of the sofa, still staring meaningfully into my eyes. For a few moments, she was silent. Then she announced, 'Wolf, with this wool you are going to make a ball.'

It must have been clear from the way I looked at her that I didn't have a clue what she was on about.

'About as big as that one there,' she said, pointing at something on a wooden shelf beside me: a pinkish-yellow ball the size of a grapefruit.

She added, looking deep into my eyes again, that it was *very relaxing*. I wondered why she thought I needed to relax, when I'd been relaxing non-stop for a year and a half. Were my own childhood experiences of education that obvious?

But without waiting for a response, she turned and walked – no, floated – back to the other side of the classroom, where she began to sing a calming song. The effect it had on me was anything but. She swayed gently back and forth as she sang, and didn't take her eyes off me for a second.

I regarded the wool, wondering whether to protest and what arguments Yvette would be most responsive to. Maybe I could go for a reminder that it was Nina's first day and I'd been hoping to observe her – to make sure there wasn't anyone here undergoing anti-aggression therapy, for instance. But my urge to monitor her might be interpreted as latent ill feeling, as if I suspected that something wasn't quite right with the people here, or the school – or even Saint Rudolf himself. Or would I appear to be shirking the challenge?

I didn't want to embarrass Nina. After all, we were hoping she'd be able to spend the next four months here, so it was probably wise to stay on the right side of her teachers. I decided to focus on being open-minded and take on Yvette's friendly but firm challenge.

I picked up the wool, hoping for enlightenment. It felt soft and fluffy, but that was all. Recalling my quality management training, I turned my attention to my objective. The pinkish-yellow ball that I was to take as an example was flawless: firm, smooth and perfectly symmetrical. I dropped it on the floor to test it and to my surprise, the thing didn't only look like a ball, it also behaved like one, bouncing back into my hand. Wasn't that a physical impossibility for something made of a kilo of tangled wool?

The perfection of my model did not, of course, make things any easier for me. Yvette signalled graciously to me to get going, miming wool-winding in the air with her hands. It flashed through my mind that I'd been coerced into a kind of initiation ritual or some form of psychological test; probably a combination of the two. This ball I'd been asked to make would no doubt reveal everything about me, like those Rorschach tests where, stare as I might, I generally found it hard to see anything but a certain part of the female anatomy. What would my woolly ball say about my mental health, my emotional state, my prenatal traumas, my political orientation? Would its jumbled lines reveal insufficient structure and an inability to face up to life's challenges? Rudolf Steiner knew what he was doing when he came up with this test, and Purple Yvette was sure to be a very practised woolly-ball reader.

After about ten minutes, the object slowly taking shape between my fingers was indisputably a cube. I did my best to smile a *very relaxed* smile. Then I ratcheted up the pace and added an occasional diagonal to my wool-winding. I was reminded of Gandhi, who had infuriated the stiff-as-starch British emissaries during the negotiations for India's independence by fiddling around with a spinning wheel as the fate of all those millions was decided. I was letting my thoughts distract me. Another ten minutes and I was holding a wonky egg. I stopped winding and decided I deserved a break. It was a while before I realised there was someone in front of me, clearing her throat.

I glanced up. She was about six years old, with Asian features. The left foot of her tights had a hole in it, and two long toes were sticking out. She said to me earnestly, 'That's a small ball.'

When I didn't respond, she continued severely, 'We make *big* balls.' Then she looked at me again expectantly.

Really, I ought to have been pleased that the girl was generous enough to describe my creation as a ball. But before I had a chance to reply, she spoke again, as if I were half-witted or hard of hearing. 'We make *bigger* balls,' she said – adding, as if it explained everything, 'You know,' and showing me the size of a bigger ball with her hands.

Hurriedly, I wound another strand of wool around my small, misshapen ball.

The girl nodded encouragingly. Then she seemed to decide that I was capable of completing the task by myself, and skipped off to the other children.

I sank back in relief. The AC/DC song 'Big Balls' popped into my head. For a second, I was tempted to get up on the sofa and blast the words into the room, but I didn't want poor Nina to have to explain to everyone that she'd never met that horrid man before in her life.

Yvette was calmly folding colourful silk squares into smaller colourful silk squares when the playroom door opened and a man in overalls came in, a heavy iron plate in his hands, and picked his way through the scattered wooden toys. It was John, who was working for the school. We'd already met a few times. I automatically hid my wool creation between my knees.

As our eyes met, he said, 'Hi Wolf, how's life?'

'Oh, fine, thanks,' I said, trying to make a thumbs-up sign but getting the wool caught around my sleeve.

John looked quizzically at my thighs.

'Just doing a bit of tidying up,' I said, as gravely as I could.

He nodded slowly, raising an eyebrow. But he had a 40kg metal plate in his hands, so after a quick, 'Well, good luck,' he trotted over to Yvette.

I breathed a sigh. Then, for the first time in over half an hour, I glanced across at Nina, who seemed to be settling in nicely. Currently she was one of five pregnant mountain cats who had formed a chain so that only the last of them risked being eaten by the snow monsters. Red in the face and whispering nervously to one another, the cats crept over the steep mountain ridge of toys. The monsters might appear at any second. The wind howled around the icy crests. Nothing existed for those cats beyond that one hazardous moment in the snowy mountains. Yesterday, the moment hadn't yet been dreamt up, and by tomorrow it would probably be forgotten. But here and now, there was nothing else in the world. That's part of the bliss of children's games: the moment is everything, and has no need to provide answers.

Suddenly, the scales fell from my eyes. I had probably brought the woolly-ball exercise on myself with my question to the headmaster yesterday: I sensed I was being taught that a day in kindergarten could be meaningful without competence-based learning targets and future-oriented portfolio documentation. It was enough for the kids to play in their own little world and enjoy themselves; they didn't need constant supervision to make sure they were reaching their targets. The woolly ball was my opportunity to re-establish the trust between the parent and the school, from the alpha to the omega. I went back to winding wool as if my life depended on it. Now that I'd understood that the meaning of this purposeless activity was to teach me that things can be meaningful without having a purpose, I found it much easier.

After another 20 minutes or so of highly focused work, I held something new in my hands. In the end, it looked like a very floppy three-legged cow with a ridiculously full udder. I looked around me anxiously for the girl who had given me such helpful advice, but she had just been caught by a snow monster and hadn't noticed my plight.

Then I was granted mercy. Yvette floated over to me and took the unfortunate cow out of my hands. She held it up to the light that streamed in through the windows behind me.

Now it was coming. She was going to explain all about meaningful purposelessness and the eternal moment.

'A ball is a ball is a ball, isn't it?' I said quickly, hoping to beat her to it by getting straight to the philosophical essence of it all.

She smiled and turned my failed ball over and over in her hands. 'Actually, I'd say that a cow is a cow is a cow,' she said with a wink. 'Oh well, it's all just a game, isn't it?'

She was right, but I realised that the school was growing on me. If Yvette was able to recognise my inner cow, I felt sure she'd get along very well with Nina. Plus there were no metal fire engines lying around. As for Atlantis, well… Nina would probably be delighted to hear about human beings and mountain cats setting off from the island all those years ago. It was just another parallel universe. According to the curriculum, fairies were also regular visitors at the school. What more could you want?

When we returned home after our eventful morning, Vera and Mr Simon were sitting on the veranda. First they were given a detailed description of the tough life of a mountain cat. Mr Simon was visibly impressed. And then, when the initial storm of words was over, Nina piped up. 'Daddy made a little pink cow!'

I nodded. I could hardly deny it.

'And did you get to grips with the learning targets?' Vera asked.

'Yup,' I said, with as much self-assurance as I could muster. 'A journey is a dream is an adventure is life is a journey. That's the learning target.'

'I knew you'd get there in the end,' Vera said.

'Child's play!' I said.

# REAL MEN

MANY WOMEN WHO TRAVEL TO AUSTRALIA NEVER quite make it back. It isn't that they plan to emigrate; they come for the university vacation or after clocking up enough overtime to stay for a month or so. But then, like my friend Steffi from Freiburg, they arrive home six days late, blushing and mumbling something about a delayed plane. They seem livelier than usual and eventually it all comes out: they've met Mat or Dan or John. Mat or Dan or John has a decent-sized plot of land situated on some stunning stretch of coast. Back home in Germany, bemused friends gather around her phone to admire a fine figure of a man in a lumberjack shirt, photographed against a brilliant blue sky. He's at least as good-looking as Jeff Bridges or Paul Walker, only he isn't a film star. This man prefers more solid work. Mat, for example, builds houses with whatever's going, but will turn his hand to pretty much anything, even tinkering with the huge engine block of his Dodge ute. *Sure, we can fix that,* he'll say, and most of the time it's true. You could spend weeks on a sunbed without getting a tan like his – and with all that physical work, the man has no need to diet.

Mat's former schoolmate Dan is a slightly different case: he was licensed to practise law in Perth and had a smart apartment down in Cottesloe. But then his dad was taken ill and somebody had to take care of the vineyards: 40 hectares of Sauvignon Blanc and Shiraz grapes down towards the Frankland River. Dan quite literally stepped into the old man's boots – the wellies were a good fit, once he'd taken out the newspaper – and with Mat's help, he soon had the tractor up and running, too. Mat owed Dan a favour from the time he'd almost lost his driving licence; Dan, with his legal knowledge, had pointed out that the breathalyser test was invalid because the police had forgotten to switch their blue lights on.

Dan and Mat and the others, who like to refer to each other as *boys* or *mates*, are strong, silent, stoic types with big hearts. If Romeo Montague had been Australian, he'd have turned up on Lord Capulet's veranda one evening after a day's work, given the huge, fierce dog a friendly pat, rolled up the sleeves of his sweat-soaked, red-and-white checked shirt, put his hat on the table, opened two cans of frozen pale ale and said, 'Man, I really like your daughter.'

And if the keep-it-simple technique unexpectedly failed him (maybe because Lord Capulet happened to be a southern European immigrant, whose complicated old-Europe-style melancholy had yet to be mellowed by the Antipodean sun), old Rommy, as the villagers would have called him, would have left the remaining four tinnies untouched (really, Capulet could do better than that swill) and lifted an entirely complicit Jules onto the back of his ute. Then, after a quick toot on the horn – they wouldn't have hung around, knowing that the histrionic Lord Capulet was probably already hunting for cartridges for his double-barrelled shotgun – they'd have yelled, 'Eat dust!' and zoomed off the Capulet estate into the sunset to start over, a few thousand klicks away at the other end of the continent.

Men like John, Mat and Dan rate German women pretty highly, almost up there with the Swedes. German women are also considered less complicated and more hands-on than their more feminine but often perplexing French counterparts. You can't manage a few hectares of land by dreaming of Paris every evening, as Dan once told me, man to man, after I'd given a rather-too-long and rather-too-uncritical monologue on the subject of Sophie Marceau. I don't know how many times Australian men congratulated me on having *landed* Vera – 'Well done, mate' – or casually inquired whether she might have a sister waiting in the wings.

\* \* \*

We had been travelling through a country of international marriages. Germans and Australians seemed to hit it off particularly well, but other countries, too, from Canada to Japan, were evidently happy to lose their daughters to Australian men. The village of Rosewood Bay, awash with Mats and Dans and Johns, was a kind of permanent United Nations gathering, and a highly productive one.

Watching John in action, I was able to see first-hand how Australian men pull this off without really doing anything at all. John had studied electrical technology at university and then set up a small business with his younger brother, making bespoke barbecues. Barbecuing is sacred in Australia; I'm sure UNESCO World Cultural Heritage status is already pending – after all, the Germans managed to get their tooth-breaking bread added to the list. John and his brother weren't exactly raking it in, but they were doing all right. Their business cards had begun to do the rounds of Perth's wealthy, and since then the boys had been able to put a bit back for the houses they were planning to build. Most of the barbecues commissioned by the well-off lawyers, estate agents and businessmen of Perth were overambitious, oversized monsters that weren't as likely to be user-friendly, but the rich Perthians tended not to listen to John's warnings. They insisted on their grotesque fantasy barbecues and John ended up welding the things together exactly as they wanted; they'd end up so heavy it took a small lorry to transport them. The day before John met Professor Steffi Wittlich from Freiburg, however, he'd had the day off from making barbecues and had at last found time to finish his almost-four-metre-high swing. He'd made it using a beam that had been washed ashore when a Chinese freight ship was wrecked 30km off the coast. Much more fun than creating those posh fake barbies, he told the professor with a twinkle in his eye.

The professor had come to stay with us after a trip to Perth. Vera and I were always glad of visitors after 18 months on the road. John's sister had asked us to dinner, so we took her along with us.

The new swing turned out to be so sturdy that the frame didn't budge a millimetre when the professor sat on it.

Once she was on, John grabbed her by the hips to pull her back and give her a good push. She gave him a look that made my blood run cold. You didn't mess with Steffi. Still only in her mid-30s, she already had a lectureship in macroeconomics at a prestigious university and ran a largely male business of more than 50 employees. I wasn't even sure that she and John had been introduced yet. But just as I was thinking that John was going to get a full-on feminist lecture, he gave her a friendly wink, pulled the swing even higher and let go. The professor was silent except for a quiet *wheee!*

Two evenings later we met up with John and his family and a few friends for a picnic. High-frequency picnicking is one of the most delightful hobbies of the West Australian female. The male version is practised at a slight distance and involves standing by the shore with your mates and staring at the horizon, a can of beer in your hand. Rosewood Bay is well situated for this with some of the most beautiful beaches in the world right on its doorstep, any one of which is unforgettable.

If you drive out of Rosewood through the coastal hills, on the dusty red roads that have to be bulldozed clear of macchia vegetation every year, you eventually come to a sandy beach between Denmark and Walpole. The water there is so clear that even 150 metres from the shore you can still see every shell on the soft white sand of the seabed. That would be paradise enough, but there is more nearby: another beach where ice-cold fresh water gushes out of the rocks in the shimmering heat, and not far from there, a cove where (accompanied, if you're lucky, by majestic rays) you can swim about in a kind of labyrinth of huge reddish-brown rocks, polished smooth by the sea. Some of these rocks lie just below the surface, so it looks as if you are walking on water.

On our first visit to the cove, I tried this trick on Nina, hoping to impress her, but she only nodded calmly and murmured, 'Finally.' It was there, too, that our flying practice began to yield results. For the first time, I managed to fling her up into the air so high that she was able to stretch her imaginary wings right out, spreading her fingers like a bird of prey splaying its feathers. And for a moment, she flew. Instead of falling straight back down, she seemed to hang in the air for a split second – a tiny fraction of the lifetime of a soap bubble.

Nina thought I should consider taking up flying assistance professionally. To be going on with, she generously offered to lend me to all the other children on the beach, who eagerly took her up on her offer. I added *flying assistant* to the list of potential jobs in my journal.

I'd often wondered who named the world's beaches. Beneath *flying assistant*, I wrote *namer of beaches*. I saw myself sitting around on nameless beaches, listening to the sea until a name came to me. We sometimes spent whole afternoons doing nothing but driving aimlessly along the dusty coastal roads between Peaceful Bay and Albany, marvelling at what we saw. Just looking at a landscape can make you feel happy. In my journal, I added another item to the list headed *Aspects of Paradise*: *landscapes that never stop (in space and time)*. On one such afternoon, we began to ooh and aah as we came over a hill, and Vera gradually slowed the car until we came to a halt in a cloud of dust in the middle of the road. Then we just looked at each other, laughing speechlessly, because we didn't have the words to describe such beauty. The sea before us was painted in a whole palette of blues, from cobalt to cerulean, and the rocks shone dark red in the sun. The sand was almost white; the dense coastal vegetation, flattened by the wind, was a washed-out blue-green. The sea pressed itself onto the shores of a little island and up against either side of a narrow sandbank, where the crystal-clear waves rolled into each other and broke like liquid glass. Even Nina had nothing to say. We had never seen anything like that bay in our lives, and I swore at that moment never to write down its name – my first professional secret as a namer of beaches.

*   *   *

Given the beauty of our surroundings, there was nothing weird about wanting to finish off the day with your feet in the water and a can of beer in your hand, and it's what we menfolk were doing on the evening of the picnic. Or rather, it's what John and his mates were doing; I'd fetched myself an ice cream from the cool box. This was greeted with raised eyebrows, but the boys and I had already discussed our differences at length and agreed to disagree. So there we were, staring with manly intent at the horizon, when suddenly John asked, 'How's Sweetie?'

'Who?'

'Your friend from Germany,' John said, looking at me expectantly.

I'd better warn him, I thought. 'She's coming later with Vera. Listen John, Sweetie's a macroeconomics professor and runs a company of 50 men.'

'Sweet,' John replied.

'So whatever you do, don't call her Sweetie,' I said, persevering. 'It doesn't work like that in Germany.'

'Doesn't work like what?'

'Well, for one thing, it's best if you don't grab a woman you don't know by the hips.'

John looked at me with a frown. 'Thanks, Doctor. At last some advice on how to handle women.'

'I'm only telling you how it is. You're better off waiting until she's made it clear it's what she wants. Same goes for holding doors for her, helping her into her coat, giving her advice, waving her into a parking space, carrying her suitcase and all that.'

John looked bemused. 'Really?'

'You shouldn't simply assume that girls can't manage by themselves.'

'And what if it's a really heavy suitcase?' John cracked his knuckles.

He had a point; I'd often secretly wondered the same. 'You have to give her a chance to carry it herself, if that's what she wants,' I said weakly.

Without understanding it all myself, I did my best to set forth the essence of European feminism as persuasively as possible. After a rather lengthy monologue, I searched John's face for a spark of understanding.

'So, I'm supposed to stand there, watching her struggle with her suitcase without lifting a finger,' he said drily.

'Yeah, that's about the size of it,' I said. 'Wait until she asks for your help.'

'Complicated,' said John.

'Wolfi,' said Dan, joining the debate, 'a man has to do what a man has to do.' He gave me a meaningful stare.

I caught my breath. There wasn't a trace of irony in his face. A few of the other lads nodded in agreement and gazed out at the horizon again. I couldn't believe these men's staggering trust in their own firm grasp of things – never mind their firm grasp on the hips of female professors.

'If you ask me, not offering to help a woman is totally unmasculine.' John's voice tore me from my thoughts.

'What's masculine, then, in your opinion?' I asked defiantly.

'Not wearing a wetsuit to drink beer?' Dan said, and John chuckled.

I looked down at myself. I was still wearing the three-millimetre-thick wetsuit. At that time of year, the seawater was well under 20 degrees. The others were standing there in their trunks; clearly it was not the done thing to wear a wetsuit, but the last time I'd tried it I'd caught a nasty cold. The drinking-beer-in-the-water lark can go on until you've lost all sensation in your legs, if not from the cold water, then from the beer. But of course, I wasn't even drinking beer; I was standing there with half an almond Magnum in my hand.

I knew from talking to my Aussie mates that culturally they thought I was a bit of a freak, and maybe even wondered on occasion whether I was some kind of different species. Not only did I suffer from chronic classical-musical-family-itis; I also showed every symptom of acute metrosexuality. According to Dan, this came 'pretty close to gayish', though he was keen to assure me that he didn't mean it was bad to be gay – 'Ab-so-lute-ly not.' So it was a good thing, I thought, that they didn't know about my secret yoga habit. Who knows what they'd have said if they'd seen me performing downward dogs on the veranda. It had not escaped their attention that I was anti-alcohol, or that I had an advanced chocolate addiction and an unmasculine incapacity for manual work; the mud bricks I had made were an exception. They knew that I owned no land, and they had discovered that I thought cricket was a game you played from a horse. Worst of all, I had an academic title but seemed to be out of work, and could be observed scribbling in my journal at inappropriate moments. I also spent a striking amount of time engaged in weird earthy activities with a self-declared part-time extraterrestrial and her little brother.

It was clear that to someone like Dan – someone who believed that a man has to do what a man has to do – such a way of life could appear complicated. There were moments when I wouldn't have minded a more straightforward life myself. Something along the lines of land, wife, mud, brick, home, kids and sea. Why not? I could see the attraction. Luckily, the boys were patient with Wolfi, as they liked to call me. I'd last been called that by my grandma when I was eight, but somehow it felt right. I felt secure in their robust, teasing company in a way that was new to me. But I really mustn't let them find *that* out.

'Yeah, it is a bit complicated,' I admitted. 'Anyone else for a choc ice on a stick with crunchy almond pieces?'

They shook their heads affectionately. It's good to find people who show you how to laugh at yourself.

\* \* \*

When Vera and Sonja turned up with Professor Wittlich in tow, she and John finally got round to official introductions.

'Sorry, what was your name again?' the professor asked.

'I'm John,' said John, politely squeezing her hand, 'but you can call me Sweetie, if you like.'

I flinched. The professor giggled.

'Pleasure,' she said, beaming all over her face. 'I'm Stefanie, but you can call me Steffi.' The two of them looked long and hard at each other – and then for a little longer. I'm pretty sure that from that moment, there was no stopping their relationship; that Steffi's delayed flight back was already sealed by fate.

Later that evening I received a rather mysterious invitation from Dan and the other boys. They seemed to have been conferring among themselves while I was checking up on the kids, because when I rejoined them, they raised their cans of beer in sync and stared silently at the horizon. Then, after furtive glances and almost imperceptible nods, Dan asked me to meet them down by the old railway bridge at the mouth of the Rosewood River the following Saturday at six in the morning. They were going to *do* something. I'd need sports clothes and a towel. That was as much information as they'd give me – no, there was one more thing: I could leave my wetsuit at home.

I promised to be punctual, but wondered what it could all mean. What did a bunch of Australian guys get up to at 6am at the old railway bridge? Did they lift sleepers? Fish for dynamite? Spar? Was it going to be another initiation ritual like at the Steiner school? I wondered whether Nina's kneepads would fit me and wished I had a mouthguard.

When Saturday morning dawned, I found seven or eight men in tracksuits lined up along the river in the dim morning light, evidently warming up. Thick mist still hung over the inlet and the river. Rosewood Bay was asleep. I spotted Dan through the mist. He introduced me to a man at the front who seemed to be the one issuing instructions.

'This is Tom. We call him Swami Tom for fun,' Dan announced. 'We're the Rosewood RaYs. Running and Yoga – get it? Today we're only doing yoga, because some of us have to leave early. The Mysore Ashtanga series. It's kind of strenuous, but it comes with time.' He patted me on the back. 'Look at it as a kind of trial run, eh?'

I nodded and found a spot behind a man who was doing a slightly skew-whiff downward dog, with trembling arms and a bright red face.

'Hey, John,' I said when I recognised him.

'Hey, Wolfi,' he groaned.

'I didn't have you down as a yoga guy,' I said, unable to resist.

He didn't miss a beat. 'A man has to do what a man has to do.' He was upside down and it was still pretty dark, but I was sure I saw a twinkle in his eyes.

# YOU NEVER RUN ALONE

IT WOULD HAVE BEEN A SENSATION IF ALONSO HADN'T made that crucial error on the third south bend at the Malaysian Grand Prix.

'Looks like Alonso didn't see Vettel's attack coming,' the commentator whined. 'Something went very wrong indeed. Now, in the last lap, this could be the big chance Vettel has been waiting for. Alonso, safely in the lead for the first half of the race, and now – what a goof!' A breathless pause. Then the same radio-style voice but at full volume, half an octave higher and with twice the pace: 'Vettel's risking everything now, with no regard for the consequences – and, ladies and gentlemen, can you believe it, he's overtaken Alonso, he's actually done it, straight past him on that final bend, and now he's leading by half a length on the home straight! Incredible! The spectators are going wild! They're jumping up and down! This could be the decisive moment – is it victory for Vettel? Is it…?'

I paused and cleared my throat. Glancing at Nina next to me on the patio, I was pleased to see that I had carried it off this time. According to Nina, there were three levels I could reach in the games we played. At Level 1, she would complain that I didn't sound *quite real*. 'Come on, Dad, be *realitsic*!' That was a polite but damning verdict: it meant that my enthusiasm was palpably half-hearted, and Nina made it clear that she had no use for me if my heart wasn't in it. I knew I'd fared better if she said rather patronisingly that I'd *done well* or was even *really realitsic*. That was Level 2 and meant that I had performed respectably, given that I was only a grown-up and could hardly be expected to do better. But it still wasn't enough to engage Nina. She'd watch me sitting there next to what we had reimagined as a racetrack or a fortress or stables or whatever, waving my arms about, but she wasn't really *in* the game – only mildly amused, like a professional theatre director watching an amateur actor reel off his lines without properly inhabiting the role.

This time, though, I had clearly reached Level 3. Level 3 meant *real*. With shining eyes and her hands clenched, Nina was staring, rapt, at Vettel, the darker of the two snails – or had I mixed them up? Hadn't Vettel been paler yesterday, and perhaps a little slimmer, too?

Relieved, I abandoned the commentary. Sustaining it at that level of intensity was pretty exhausting, shrieking away for minutes on end without pausing for breath, and now that Nina was *in* the game, it was no longer necessary. We watched in silence as Vettel slimed his way over the white chalk mark ahead of Alonso. A sensational slow-motion triumph. Soundless, too. Snails are quiet winners.

To my astonishment, Nina said nothing. Usually, at this point she would say something regretful like, 'That was quick.' Or, taking a more pragmatic approach, she would try to pin down the next activity. 'And now let's do…'

But today, she was as mute as Vettel. The look on her face told me that something was up. I waited. Halfway through tidying chalk and racecourse-fence twigs into a yoghurt pot, I heard her voice behind me.

'Vettel was quicker.'

There was something strange about her tone, and the remark was hardly necessary, as Vettel's triumph had been incontrovertible. I turned to face her. She was holding Alonso tightly in her fist. She always did this, though I'd tried to tell her not to. It could take almost ten minutes' scrubbing with soap to get the slime off her. The snail was peeping out of her fingers, his eye-stalks protruding, so either he was extremely relaxed (unlikely), or Nina was squeezing too tightly (all too probable). I was about to suggest tentatively that it might be a good idea to loosen her grip when she held Alonso up to my face. He was so close that I had to squint to get him in focus.

'Alonso lost again,' she said gloomily.

That wasn't exactly news, either. But the truth was beginning to dawn on me: Nina was starting to feel sympathy for the losers. Her eyes were as deep as the sea.

'Maybe he'll win tomorrow,' she said, and it didn't sound like a question or even conjecture, more like an order to make sure it happened: to rig the next race, if necessary. While I'd been busy tidying up the racetrack, she had come up with a way to make losing bearable: if everyone could take it in turns to win, all would be well again.

I swallowed. What Nina was asking of me with her snail was a kind of compensatory justice, a way of getting things back on an even keel, of scripting a happy ending that satisfied everyone.

'You never know,' I conceded. 'Maybe Alonso *will* win tomorrow.' Even as I said it, I felt guilty. It wasn't the first time I'd fudged things against my better judgement, and it never helped. Fudging things only ever made them worse.

\*   \*   \*

In my journal, I made some notes on the subject of losing. It seemed to me that losing is one of life's essential experiences, especially given the current climate in which winning is so exalted. There's an entire industry feverishly working away to promote the concept of the winner. Look closely at sports programmes or celebrity magazines and you see the message: *there can be only one winner. The winner takes it all*, for instance, or *nothing's sexier than success*. The one that really got to me was *better dead than second*. Even worse, all this fantastic winner stuff is churned out with some large-scale fudging to stop the losers from feeling like losers. It's unconscionable: first we're told there can only be one winner and that all the losers might as well drop down dead and then, in the same breath, the losers are told, *taking part is everything!* or, *the journey is the goal*, or, *it's all a question of training and protein shakes.* No wonder people feel hard done by when they go to the cinema and aren't rewarded with a happy ending where the lame get up and walk and the blind can see. Only very old French directors are allowed to make sad films these days, gloom being the reserve of suburban arthouse cinemas.

When someone is disabled, though, there is basically no fudging the issue. Just because you're not good at one sport, it doesn't mean you'll be good at another. Nina was almost always one of the last – in running *and* climbing *and* swimming *and* throwing *and* catching. She was always the last to be picked for a team, unless a grown-up had given her a head start or two extra lives. Who knew, maybe Alonso would never be as fast as Vettel. And no, if sport wasn't your thing, it didn't mean you got to be a maths genius instead. That was a subtler form of fudging: the idea that Nina had to be great at something. Did she? *Really?* Other parents, wanting to be supportive, would say things like, 'She'll get there in the end,' or, 'She's really come on in the last six months.' I think this was very closely related to the kinds of thoughts I had when I was still Curitiba Man and hoped that things would 'get better one day'. Then there were the sentences ending with the word *considering.* Every time, I wanted to ask, 'Considering *what*, exactly?' It was as if there had to be some form of compensation, as if justice had to be done. Another good one was the *still, she does* sentence: 'Still, she does speak fluent English now'… 'Still, she does have the most incredible imagination.' Yes, true enough. But why *still* ? And if ever I said, no, there was very little chance that things *would* improve as she got older, I was sometimes told, 'Oh, wait and see,' as if I were being irrationally pessimistic. It gave me an odd feeling, too, when close friends or relatives said, 'It's fine the way it is.' Because that, too, was a kind of fudging. Losing is sad. Sad for Nina. Actually, it is what it is.

Of course, they wanted to help, and they probably sensed my

pain. Watching a loved one lose almost tears your heart out. It does mine, anyway.

* * *

Shortly before we set off on our travels, Nina ran a race over a big lawn with a few other kids. The children, naturally, hadn't been content just to play. Children, especially boys, seem to be genuinely competitive creatures. They always have to compare themselves to others: they have to know who can run fastest, climb highest, dive deepest, jump furthest. And Nina – Little Miss *Swow* herself, who had influenced me to leave pretty much every one of life's races – was determined to join in. It was completely incomprehensible to me. Why did she keep doing it? Why did she continue to put herself in situations where she could only lose?

I tried to persuade the kids to do something else. 'Oh, come on,' I said, 'you don't always need to be racing each other. Let's play a different game.'

But they were so excited that they didn't even hear me. They were already organising themselves into a more-or-less straight line, the two boys exchanging last-minute insults. (It's all part of competing.) My heart began to thud as they stormed off, screeching.

The whole thing was over in perhaps ten seconds, and Nina came last, although there were considerably younger children taking part. Even halfway across the lawn she was far behind the others, as if she were running the race on her own. There was something almost lonely about the way she lurched across the lawn, body tilted forwards, arms stretched out, staggering so heavily from side to side that I kept thinking she was about to fall. I could hardly bear to watch. By the time she reached the finishing line, the other kids were already moving on to the next activity. I saw Nina wander about among them, panting. I can still see her now. It is one of hundreds of such scenes, but it stands out from the others because I felt her pain – a loved one's pain – so acutely that day.

* * *

A conspiratorial mumbling brought me back to the patio. I glanced at Nina, who was telling Alonso she was sure he'd win tomorrow. Alonso remained silent.

How was I going to convey to Nina the three difficult messages that had been included in Dr Finkelbach's groundbreaking report?

1.  This is how it is.

2.  It is difficult.

3.  This is how it's going to stay.

I couldn't do it. It wasn't the truth, as such, that was the problem. The problem was that the truth offered no consolation. I quite simply had no idea how to comfort Nina without resorting to fudging.

Other people teach their children how to win. The coordinator of a UNEP task force recently posted a photo of his son holding a golf club almost bigger than himself. When he was two, his father told me he had hired a Chinese nanny 'to make him fit for a globalised world'. But while top-paid consultants were initiating competitiveness in tender-aged children at international elite schools, here I was with a yoghurt pot full of racing snails, wondering how to teach a six-year-old how to lose. Wasn't it too much for a child, however brave?

\* \* \*

A few days after Vettel's triumph, I was given the chance to test myself. How good a loser was I? In theory, losing wasn't a problem for me. I never minded losing at ludo, for instance. But now, for the first time since I'd joined the RaYs, there was to be a real race. So far we had only jogged casually along the Heritage Trail by the inlet, startling the occasional black swan. We didn't care who was fastest; all we wanted was to cover the distance and have fun together. As far as I was concerned, it could have stayed that way. But then Ben, a very good runner, started interval training with us, and it was decided that this should culminate in a 3km race. We arranged to meet at the sports ground.

Of course, when Nina and Mr Simon got wind of it, they were desperate to come along and watch me race.

'It's best if you stay here with Mum. I'm sorry to disappoint you, kids, but the other RaYs are really fast runners and have been training for much longer than me,' I told them. Besides, I was aiming low. In fact, I was more interested in losing and how that would feel. Maybe I would develop greater empathy for my daughter.

I overheard Nina boasting to her friends about my putative heroism, and knew that the kids wanted to feel proud of their dad.

'Please let us come,' she begged the evening before the race. 'We'll clap for you.'

But I remained firm.

I ran the race calmly, almost making a point of lagging behind the others. I started off neck-and-neck with Robert, but soon lost sight of him. I might have managed to overtake Swami Tom, who seemed to be having a bad day, but I didn't bother trying. I ran with my head held high, feeling almost triumphant at having nothing to prove to anyone. And it worked. It turned out I didn't mind losing at all. It simply required a shift in mindset.

When I rolled up at the finishing line with almost exaggerated calm, Swami Tom was leaning against a goalpost, panting heavily. 'You're last?' he asked.

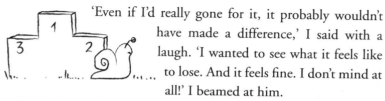
'Even if I'd really gone for it, it probably wouldn't have made a difference,' I said with a laugh. 'I wanted to see what it feels like to lose. And it feels fine. I don't mind at all!' I beamed at him.

Maybe I was hoping for praise, but Swami Tom is quite the philosopher. He snorted into his T-shirt and chuckled at me.

'What are you laughing at?' I felt he wasn't taking me seriously.

'To be honest, it looked more like you didn't even try. That's fake, Wolfi.'

I looked at him in annoyance. He was still panting.

'So if you *really* want to know what it's like to lose, maybe you should actually try to win!'

Our eyes met. He raised his eyebrows and then pulled his hoodie over his head so that it partly covered his face. Ben and John were already waiting at the exit, as Ben had to be at work by half past eight and if we wanted to make our usual stopover at our favourite café, we had to get going.

I stood irresolutely in front of Swami Tom, still uncertain how to react. I felt caught out. Sometimes I had the impression that it amused him to watch me puzzling over decisions and making the wrong ones – stumbling through my trial-and-error life. He jerked his head towards our parked cars and I nodded. As we bumped along the street in his enormous truck, neither of us said a word.

*    *    *

About three weeks later, John and Ben sounded the horn outside our house at ten on a Saturday morning, as they did every weekend. After three sessions of interval training, we were going to run 4km. I was less than keen. Ben had announced that he'd be setting a particularly brisk pace. John, for some reason, wanted to run barefoot, which he claimed wasn't a problem on grass. I gathered up my trainers, water bottle and towels, and went to the back door of the cottage. Nina and Mr Simon were playing on the patio with a city of Playmobil and sticks. The bricks underfoot were already warm from the sun. I wouldn't normally have disturbed their game, but today I had a plan.

'Mupples?' I called – my pet name for them.

'Yes?' they piped in unison, their two blond heads swivelling round.

'Come with me. We're going to the sports ground. I want to show you something.'

'You're going to race!' said Nina. She clapped her hands, and Mr Simon joined in.

At the ground there was an atmosphere of intense excitement. From a miniature spectators' stand of staggered stone blocks, two little voices called, 'Da-ddy, Da-ddy, Da-ddy,' breaking off to giggle every few seconds. I felt queasy. Even Swami Tom had given me a questioning look when I turned up with the kids, the only one of us to bring any. We RaYs positioned ourselves along the starting line, jostling noisily. Although it was only for fun, I could see the tension in everyone's faces. Ben and John were snapping at each other, half in earnest. (It's all part of competing.) Then everyone fell silent. The lull before the start was almost unbearable.

'On your marks!' Ben called.

'Get set!'

Close your eyes and go for it, I told myself.

'Go!' Ben roared, fiddling with the buttons on his watch.

And the race began.

Ben and John shot into the lead after setting off at a ridiculous pace. I didn't see how anyone could keep running that fast. I had to cut my speed considerably after only half a lap and watch the others sail past me. About 100 metres further on, I looked across at Nina and Mr Simon. Their arms were already hanging by their sides; Mr Simon had stopped cheering me on, but Nina kept it up. She would. It hurt. All of a sudden, I realised that the pain coursing through me was the same pain I felt when *she* was losing: the pain of the defeat of a loved one – only this time the defeat was my own.

But this wasn't the time to start philosophising, and I continued to run as fast as I could. From the other side of the track, the kids' faces were a blur. They were both sitting there in silence now. It felt terrible. What had I let myself in for? And what was I inflicting on *them*? Something inside me was screaming to give up. Right now. I longed to stroll coolly over to the pair of them and say, 'Bother, my shoelaces came undone.' I came very close to it. But what was the point? I gritted my teeth and carried on running. Another lap. This time they looked at me with big eyes as I approached them. Or was I imagining things? It probably looked like I was running the race on my own. I expect I looked almost lonely.

After about three kilometres, I could taste iron, familiar to me from the Federal Youth Games in Germany, where I had once failed by a few points to win a certificate of honour. Unlike the honourless winners' certificates, which were undistinguished black-and-white photocopies, the certificates of honour were printed on thick sand-coloured paper with a seal and the president's signature, a little like the certificates that had adorned Dr Finkelbach's walls.

After 3,200 metres, I felt sick. Still another two laps to go. I ran past the kids one last time. Simon was banging the heels of his trainers against the stone he was perched on: left, right, left, right. He looked bored; 4km is a long time. I struggled the final 100 metres to the finishing line. I couldn't manage a final sprint, but kept up the pace until the last 50 metres, which I ran in big, slow strides. By the time I reached the finishing line, I was knackered, my legs trembling, the sweat pouring off me. Not only had I come last, but it was also quite clear that I'd bitten off more than I could chew. The others were already busy with shoes and towels, but when I finally staggered over to them, Swami Tom turned to me and said, 'Ah, Wolfi, welcome to the RaYs! Your probationary period is over!'

I studied his face. He was looking at me gravely, but I thought I saw him wink. Or was I seeing things? Then the others came over and gave me high fives. I felt quite touched.

But there was something I still had to do. I mumbled excuses, picked up my kit and jogged ponderously over to Nina and Simon. They didn't call to me and only watched intently as I climbed up the stone blocks to them. Their faces spoke volumes. It was clear that I was not the only one who wished I'd been hampered by a troublesome shoelace.

'Daddy, you were the very, very last,' Nina said, and Simon gave me a funny look. He felt uncomfortable about something, but was making an effort not to let it show. Had I already indoctrinated him with the idea that his dad would always win? When does losing become a problem? At about the age of two?

'Yes,' I said.

Fact Number One. I had to face up to it, and so did the kids.

'The others are much faster, you see,' I said, sitting down beside them, and it struck me how unusual it was to be admitting my own inferiority to the children. Simon was still giving me a funny look, as if he didn't quite trust me. I felt almost sorry for him. But what good is a dad who always wins? How does that make a child feel?

'Are you sad?' Nina asked, wrapping her arms around me. Her cheek felt all warm against my sweaty neck. 'Ugh!' she said, recoiling. She wiped the sweat off her face with her T-shirt and leant her head on my shoulder. She didn't seem to mind my sweat on her hair.

Time for Fact Number Two. 'Yes, I am sad. It's quite difficult,' I replied. I'd expected her to ask that question and had thought carefully about the answer.

'Maybe you'll win next time,' Nina said. 'Like Alonso.'

'I don't think so,' I said. Fact Number Three.

I looked into two rather helpless faces. There was something familiar about their expressions. I knew how it felt to witness the defeat of a loved one. I swallowed. It wasn't easy for them, but at least they were no longer on their own.

'You never run alone, Nina. Please remember that.'

'Eh?' she said.

'Just try to remember. If you ever lose, think very hard of me in this race, OK?'

'OK,' she said cheerfully.

I breathed a sigh. *Mission accomplished.* I tried to work out what I felt myself. Relieved, mainly. But also a little desolate. Losing would never feel like winning. I reached for my kit. My T-shirt was clinging damply to my back. Losers' stories don't have soothing happy endings, that's for sure.

But just as I was about to send the children on ahead to the car where Ben and John were waiting, Nina's voice piped up. 'I love you, Daddy,' she said.

She and Mr Simon surrounded me. I knelt down and four little arms came around my neck.

It is what it is.

# THE WATERSHED

IF YOU LOOK AT NEW ZEALAND ON A GLOBE, EUROPE
is out of sight. This is because New Zealand is almost the exact antipode
of Europe. So when you leave Europe, no matter what direction you set
off in, you are automatically moving closer to New Zealand. And since
the earth is a spheroid, with no beginning and no end, the same is also
true in reverse. Wherever we travelled after New Zealand, we would –
for the first time in almost two years – be moving closer to Germany.

You might say it meant that we were on our way *back*, step by
step; but for me, New Zealand became a watershed in my personal
journey. From there on in, I experienced life differently. The journey
had already changed us all, but after New Zealand the changes felt
irreversible. Rivers do not flow upstream.

When we first arrived in Christchurch, we rented a small house on
the edge of town while we acclimatised ourselves. Only a fortnight
before, temperatures in New Zealand had, rather inconsiderately,
dropped lower than they'd been for four decades. It felt about 30
degrees colder than in Rosewood Bay. We landed at Christchurch
International Airport wearing thin linen clothes and picked our way
over roads thick with ice. Even in the town centre, we sank into snow
well over our ankles: the snowplough drivers were practically minded
people who focused on clearing the deepest snow, the DIY stores were

out of shovels and – never mind that it was the heaviest snowfall in half a century – the Kiwis were far too easy-going to be bothered by a bit of rough weather. It was Mr Simon's first snow! The children were forever sucking icicles, I was forever getting snow down my collar (*really, Daddy, I thought you'd like it*) and we were constantly soaking the kids' feet in bowls of warm water.

We had no winter clothes, of course, so we paid a visit to the Salvation Army Family Store in Papanui and bought a whole heap of things for NZ$198. (We'd kitted ourselves out in second-hand shops in Rosewood – it was, quite simply, earthier than buying new clothes.) Nina ended up with various fleece layers and I bought my first pair of French designer flares, which completely covered my shoes. Perhaps some fashion-conscious Parisian hippy had parted with his favourite bourgeois jeans here in Christchurch before setting off for the tropical climes of Cape York; maybe he'd become one of Phoenix's admirers. I found a thick padded jacket from Japan and a long-sleeved T-shirt with *Detroit Tigers* on the back in huge letters.

Then we found 'Eddie', as Nina spontaneously christened a camper van the size of a small dinosaur – over seven metres long. He was a good price. There were at least 30 camper vans on the vehicle-hire car park and the receptionist was glad of our custom, as business was obviously slow. The international Rugby Championship is not the most popular time to cruise the country's numerous beauty spots in a camper van. The mighty All Blacks hadn't won the finals since 1987, and the trauma was etched deep on the New Zealand psyche. This time they had to make it; anything less would be unbearable.

We left the house in Christchurch and set off in Eddie, wriggling our way along the winding roads of the South Island. The New Zealanders (who, for whatever reason, do most things better than the rest of the world) have set up campsites in more than 200 of the country's most beautiful spots: ten-metre-square plots of more-or-less flat land in the middle of nowhere, empty apart from two simple wooden toilet blocks. Whoever builds those toilets is well disposed towards tourists; leave the door open (which you can, because there's usually not a soul around), and more often than not you will have a spectacular view of mountains, sea, lakes and open plains. There was a limit to how long you could stay at these Department of Conservation campsites, perhaps to make sure you didn't get so attached to the place that you ended up unscrewing the wheels of your camper van and staying forever. When you leave, you deposit a few dollars for each night of your stay in little honesty boxes, just as we had at the unmanned veggie stalls in Rosewood Bay. On one occasion the box was stuffed so full of notes that I could hardly fit mine in. (That tickled me: apparently, nobody here had the time to deal with the money side of things.) We passed Kaikoura and the actual watershed of the Kaikoura range: on one side of the pass, rivers flow north-east towards the Marlborough Sounds, while on the other they run towards the Antarctic waters of the South Pacific – continuing on to Blenheim and Nelson. Each of these places alone would have been reason enough to fly halfway around the planet and stand and gaze in awe.

One afternoon, we visited the petrol station where we had bought charcoal for a barbecue a couple of days before. The owner had given me a few handfuls of very special woodchips for free, which, he said, would give our food an unforgettable taste. He was right – the taste was intense, both strange and wonderful. At the time I'd made a note of the station's opening hours, as it was likely to provide our last refuelling opportunity before we went on to Abel Tasman National Park. According to our travel guide, it was advisable to keep an eye on your fuel consumption in New Zealand if you didn't want to get stranded, and even more so in winter. The author knew his way around the country. So, on time, we arrived back there at 16:15 with relatively little petrol in the tank.

As we pulled in, I wondered why the petrol station's lights weren't on, and soon established that we were the sole fuel-interested party and, moreover, the only people there.

My German reflexes flickered with frustration at the lack of punctuality and reliability, and even Curitiba Man awoke briefly. I glared at the handwritten sign detailing the opening hours on the door of the salesroom, as if just by looking I could bring the place to life. Even the sign said they closed at 5pm! Surely no one closes a popular petrol station earlier than advertised (although my moped rental experience on Ko Yao Yai should have been a warning). So I walked around the building to see who I could find.

As I searched, I realised that something in me had changed. Inner voice number one, complaining about the unreliability of the owner (who I had praised as such a nice person) was not alone any more. Inner voice number two told inner voice number one that it was embarrassing and inappropriate to knock on the door of a deserted petrol station, and that voice number one should settle down and relax. By now I felt quite sanguine about the situation, and having found nobody at home, we finally set off in Eddie. We had just enough petrol to last us for the rest of the day and decided to park near the sea and spend the night there.

When we arrived at the beach, I spotted the petrol station owner right away. He was stood behind a small boy, both of them holding the steering lines of a dragon kite, which happily pulled its tracks in the sky.

'Hi,' I greeted them, and gestured at the long expanse of virtually empty shore. 'It's nice here.'

The man gave me a friendly nod, barely taking his eyes off the dragon.

'It's cool that you came,' I said.

Now he looked at me properly; not with suspicion, just curiosity. I sensed that he had recognised me. 'How do you mean?'

'I approve,' I said. 'You closed your petrol station so you could be here instead.'

He nodded without any sign of defensiveness. 'Yeah, that's normal around here,' he said.

There it was again. The new normal. *Of course* you prematurely close a petrol station to play with your son…

On our journey, we had been confronted with the new normal many times now. It seemed to me that the notion of normality was slowly evaporating.

Perhaps it had something to do with the *length* of our travels. We had now been away for nearly two years. The impact was tangible. How often, on my short work trips to Latin America and Africa, had I been confronted with the complete opposite of what was normal in Germany? For a few weeks or months, nothing had been the way it was at home. There was the poverty in South Africa, with townships as far as the eye could see. There were the almost surreal encounters with the indigenous people of southern Venezuela, who would never have understood me, even if I'd spoken their languages fluently; our cultures were just too different. There were the tropical research stations in the middle of the Andean rainforests where even my dollar notes had begun to grow mould; the packed streets of Nairobi; the haggling at the markets of Abidjan in the Ivory Coast, a kind of art form that had little to do with price.

Time and again I had thought to make changes in my life when I returned to Bonn from one of those trips – to introduce new routines and cast off habits that were, officially, normal but seemed strange to me when considered from a distance. For instance, I resolved to spend more time chatting to strangers in public places and sharing relaxed meals with friends; maybe working less and laughing more.

But no matter how far I travelled or what I saw, the sense that my life in Bonn wasn't any more normal than any other lifestyle that I had encountered soon faded. Whenever I came back, that same old song was still playing at full blast. It soon engulfed me, so my life continued to follow the endless score of ordinariness, *da capo* – repeat from the beginning – ad infinitum.

A few weeks after I had spotted a little boy (he couldn't have been more than ten) numbing his hunger with glue only metres from the Nairobi Hilton in Kenya where I was staying on business, my latte macchiato in Bonn tasted a tad bitter. What a hard life I had! And 32 days after emerging physically unscathed but mentally shaken from a brutal tropical storm in a one-man tent on the small, tellingly named Isla Solitaria in the middle of the raging Orinoco River in southern Venezuela, I was back at home in Bonn, complaining about our imperfect king-size mattress. After months in Ecuador, where the playful, easy-going attitude to time never failed to charm me, I would be furious when somebody in Bonn kept me waiting for 22 minutes. Almost as soon I returned home, I let the distractions of 'normal' life lull me back into a stupor. I would catch myself sitting wordlessly in front of the TV next to the woman I'd been missing like crazy for the past weeks. Things did not change and neither did I, because I never crossed the watershed. And if Nina hadn't sent us on this journey through some remote areas of Thailand, Australia and New Zealand, I would probably never would have.

* * *

This journey had been long enough to shift baselines. Had it started when I watched Dennis Niebel staggering downstairs with that box of books, *The Little Prince* on top? When our rooms began to empty? Two days before we left, when we jettisoned the last surplus items after failing to fit them into our suitcases? By the time we reached New Zealand, we had shed our skins many times over. Practically nothing was left of the things we'd packed in Bonnto take with us. The first pairs of shoes had been weeded out long ago and my expensive belt had got left behind on Ko Yao Yai as part of a swing (a rather fine swing though, I must say).

When we stocked up at the Salvation Army store in Papanui, we knew that hardly any of the things we bought were for keeps. 'We'll donate everything we've bought back to you in ten weeks at the latest,' we said. The woman at the till simply nodded. People and things came and went. What did it mean under such circumstances to refer to *my* jacket?

During the beach months on Ko Yao Yai with neither razor nor mirror, I ended up losing sight of my own image – the idea that I was supposed to look a certain way. There was no need for uniforms or masks or poses of any kind, and that bass note of posturing and pretence died away. Why bother with a dress code at all? By the time we made our entry into the Prince Palace Hotel under the disapproving eye of the porters, three months after we left Bonn, we'd already given up on it.

It was similar with my inner time. The metronome of everyday life had gradually become inaudible. First the mechanical tick of my Piaget had fallen silent. That had set my inner time free. Then the workaday rhythms slowed and stopped: the constant switch between work and leisure, the inexorable beat of supermarket (and petrol station) closing times, nursery opening hours, project deadlines, application deadlines – the allegedly normal, even inevitable, 24/7 time. How was it normal for sleep to be interrupted by an alarm every morning, or to order takeaway pizza for delivery to the Institute when I worked late on a Saturday evening? How could it ever have felt normal when Vera and I arrived home from our busy jobs in the evenings and asked each other 'How was your day?' – as if our life together had been reduced to a kind of daily speed-dating session? If closeness between partners is measured in the number of minutes they spend together, how many couples would that leave in a long-distance relationship?

What did normal holidays feel like? We got 28 days a year if we worked five days a week. Aha, so holidays were originally working days, too.

Another question struck me: what's the linguistic opposite of free time?

In Thailand, the days of the week had started to blur, and when we'd reached Queensland, even the date no longer meant anything to us. Now I was wonderfully out of time – I was so many months from home that even the biggest clocks were too far away to hear. Had I really once planned my life around work appointments?

Why had I adopted the mainstream idea that you save money but have no time to spare? In South Korea, workers start with 15 days of annual leave, which increases to 25 days when they've been working for 22 years. Spanish workers typically work 11-hour days, from 9am to 8pm, with a mid-afternoon siesta. Why was it normal to discuss retiring at 70-72 in Germany, while the Swedish were considering the feasibility of a five-hour working day? Why is a man considered a 'dropout' because he wants to share his time with his family? Had I been a 'dropin' when I was never at home? Why had it been normal to leave my family at home for 30 weeks of the year so I could go on business trips? Some of the biggest companies in the world now offer to sponsor women to freeze their eggs, so that they can prioritise their careers. Buddies of mine would bring their half-awake kids to school in the morning, and the next time they saw them they'd be asleep in bed. Everywhere in the world, little kids have to get up too early, in the dark, to be parked at a breakfast club because their parents have to go to work. And then they are stored at afterschool clubs, where learning is unlikely, because their parents still aren't back from work.

* * *

By the time we arrived in Port Douglas in Queensland, my working life and the country we used to call home felt like a distant memory. A German number on my mobile display had become a rarity. It was as if, back in Germany, my number had gradually faded from people's contact lists, digit by digit. After two weeks of driving around the South Island in Eddie, I had received only two missed calls, but never in my life had I felt I was missing less.

For a long time, my subconscious must have silently clung on to the sense that our normal life was in Germany. That was the gold standard – our journey was the surreal exception. Even some weeks ago, I had remarked 'how far away' we were to Vera. Far away from what, actually? We were here now, and we had not been in Bonn for nearly two years. So why were we *away*?

We made friends on the road quickly, but generally for days and weeks rather than months, and we parted with a *maybe see you again sometime*. The time we might spend with these new friends could be intense, exploring the natural world together, sitting around or just playing. Was that friendship? On the campsites we had 24-hour neighbours. Why had we ever thought it normal to stay in one place? To have entire rooms for storing things that you obviously didn't need? Spare toilets?

The further we travelled, the weirder the concept of the normal became. Now we really questioned the statement that something was 'normal'.

So when my watershed moment hit me, here on the beach with the petrol station owner and his son, I stared at the horizon and thought to myself: if every place has its *own* normal, this makes normality a paradox. What a loudmouth normality is. She masquerades herself as a universal being, but she's just a provincial fiction! Bananas with no seeds, fish that can't fly, the earth being a disc, petrol stations that are open all the time, fathers and mothers coming home from earning money only when the children are already asleep are all considered completely normal at one time or place or another.

I did the maths in my journal later:

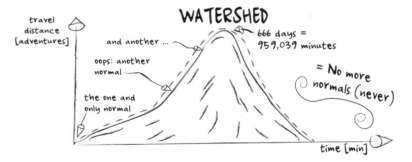

'So what are you doing here?' The voice of the man on the beach interrupted my thoughts.

'I was trying to get some petrol at your station.'

'Ah,' he said.

We both laughed. It felt good. I felt I was finally on the right side of the watershed.

'Come back tomorrow,' he said. 'Or are you in trouble? I do have a spare can with me.'

'No need, thanks. But maybe we can invite you to our barbecue? We even have special woodchips that make steaks taste like grilled turtles' armour!'

He grinned. 'Now that sounds fantastic!'

# HOME SWEET HOME

'WE'LL HAVE TO GO HOME SOON,' I SAID. DUSK WAS falling and I didn't fancy stumbling down the rocky paths with the children in the dark.

'Where?'

'Home.'

'Where is home?'

'Good question,' I said – my standard response when I didn't have an answer handy. I wasn't in the mood for a long philosophical discussion and I wanted to get going. So I added, 'What I meant was: we need to get back to Eddie.'

'Oh,' said Nina doubtfully, put out that I hadn't answered her good question.

We drifted about the island with Eddie as our mobile base camp. At about midday, we would leave him to go on dangerous mountaineering expeditions – bold adventure people, climbing hills that no man had climbed before, naming beaches and crossing rivers. In the evenings, we staggered back, exhausted, and vanished into Eddie's belly to cook and rest. It seemed natural to speak of him as *home*; I'd said it without really thinking about it.

But Nina wasn't satisfied with my explanation.

'Home is in Bonn with Grandma and Grandad,' she said.

I knew what she meant. Whenever we spoke to people back in Germany, they spoke of home. Home was very closely related to the notion of *coming back* to our allegedly normal lives, perhaps also because geographically we couldn't move any further away. In Germany, everybody seemed to assume that *home* meant the same to us as it did to them – that Bonn was the fixed point around which our lives revolved, like the sun at the centre of the solar system. Maybe it was also because we had started there and would eventually return. Or because we had lived there for so long. It was no coincidence that Nina had mentioned Bonn, but I wasn't going to make things too easy for her. After all, I had crossed my watershed.

'What about Simon?' I asked. 'Where's his home?'

It was a tricky one. Simon had been away from Germany for most of his life and had no memory of Bonn. At night he spoke English in his sleep, and his German was often a kind of double Dutch, with English syntax and an Australian accent. He was now two, and had never lived longer than a few months in one place. What Anna Amsel referred to as *latent nomadism*, when I had emailed her our itinerary, was the only way of life he knew. In his brief life there had been at least 20 places to which we had returned *home* in the evenings. Right now, it was a mobile home XL, extended family version.

For Nina, things were different. She had spent about four years of her life in Germany. Mathematically, the German minutes still outweighed all the others. But even she was fast becoming increasingly international. 'We're from Australia,' a smiling Nina told the nice New Zealand passport officer when we arrived in Christchurch.

Now, after a long day on Fox Glacier in Westland Tai Poutini National Park, she only screwed up her nose at my question about her brother and said nothing. But I knew I hadn't heard the last on the topic.

I was beginning to feel that I was losing my own sense of home. As we jolted along the roads in Eddie, I had plenty of time to ponder the matter. Was home even a place? Wasn't it more of a feeling?

\* \* \*

After stopping off at Fox Glacier, we headed for Lake Tekapo, south of the Southern Alps. This meant driving a long way through snowy mountains – not exactly an unmitigated pleasure, as there were several peaks that rose over 3,000 metres, including Aoraki at 3,724 metres. There was no avoiding the passes, and Eddie, apparently more of a lowland dinosaur, found them quite a struggle. It wasn't hard to see why Peter Jackson chose to shoot some of the more dramatic scenes of *The Lord of the Rings* in the Canterbury region, as the landscape was awe-inspiring.

It was getting late and we'd come off the highway onto a smaller road that led up to a mountain ridge. There were supposed to be breathtaking views over the other side, and a little restaurant at the top where we planned to stop for dinner to reward ourselves for the long drive. I'd promised Nina braised mountain goat and told her that we might even be able to camp in the mountains for a night.

We were about halfway up the narrow, winding road when we encountered two young men coming the other way in a four-wheel drive jeep with snow chains around its tyres. They made straight for us, braking just in time to avoid a head-on collision – and having stopped us in this fashion, grinning all over their faces, they cranked down a window.

'Everything's closed up there. We were the last to come down the mountain.'

I nodded distractedly, not really wanting to take on board what they were trying to tell us.

'Best if you turn back as soon as you can. It's snowing like crazy up on the tops and they won't be clearing it till tomorrow morning.'

'Thanks,' I said, trying to look grateful. The prospect of retracing our steps and finding somewhere to park up for the night wasn't enticing.

'What's happening now, Daddy?' said Nina.

'I'll tell you in a moment,' I promised.

Nina thanked them, too, and they drove off.

'I guess we have to go back the way we came,' said Vera.

I looked at the road in front of us. It didn't seem a bad place to do a three-point turn: there was a relatively large plateau to the right of the tarmac. It probably was the best option, given that there was no knowing how steep and narrow the road would get higher up; it's no fun manoeuvring a seven-metre-long monster like Eddie around hairpin bends, and I'd been driving for three hours and was getting tired.

'Would you like me to do it?' Vera asked.

'A man has to do what a man has to do,' I said with a smirk, and put Eddie into reverse. The plateau looked straightforward enough; there was no need to get out and check it.

Some jokes are best avoided in favour of hands-on research. My plateau turned out to be a ditch at least a metre deep, filled, presumably, with snow that had been shunted off the road by a snowplough. Perhaps it had even been specially dug for that purpose and every kindergarten child in New Zealand could have told me to keep well away from it. But I wasn't to know. Eddie's chassis immediately ran aground on the sloping side of the icy ditch. His back wheels couldn't get any purchase and, despite the peak torque of his powerful engine, he slipped slowly but steadily backwards for about two metres, ramming his rear end deep into the snow. There was an almighty crash as the crockery in the cupboards slid into the corners. Everyone shrieked. Even the unwakeable Mr Simon woke up and immediately began to demand chocolate.

I got out to inspect the damage. Eddie's back wheels were buried in the snow. I looked around me. The boys in the jeep had vanished. There was not a soul in sight, just the road and the mountains and the darkening sky. An hour at most until dusk.

Fitting iced-up snow chains under the twin tyres of a several-tonne camper van is a wretched job, especially when the ground is frozen solid. The woman who'd leased us Eddie had given us a quick demonstration of how to use the chains in the car park, which had taken her seconds. I didn't recall her lifting the camper van with one hand. If only I'd paid closer attention; she'd asked if I'd understood what to do and I'd said, 'Yes,' and that we weren't planning to drive cross-country. 'Sure,' she'd said, with a faraway look in her eyes, and handed over the keys.

My fingertips were aching with cold, especially under the nails, and I'd got my right middle finger trapped between the chain and the tyre – the same spot I'd injured making bricks. It crossed my mind that a camper van stuck in a ditch like this would present a great challenge for a managers' seminar. I'd have to speak to Beany about it if we ever made it off this mountain in one piece.

The passenger door opened and Vera's head popped out.

'You getting on all right?'

I blew onto my red hands and nodded. I could hear Mr Simon howling in the background.

'The kids OK?' I asked.

'Simon wants to play in the snow,' she said. 'But the heating's not working and if the pair of them get covered in snow we'll never get them warm…'

Great, I thought, and said nothing.

'There's no phone reception up here either, so looks like we're stuck here for the night,' Vera added. I'm sure she didn't mean to sound discouraging.

Another precious quarter of an hour was lost as dusk crept across the sky. I could only get the chains over the wheels on one side, but it turned out to be irrelevant: it seemed that Eddie was unconscious. I turned the key in the ignition several times. Not a peep. Not a single light on the dashboard. I laboriously dug the exhaust pipe out of the frozen ground, and gouged earth, grass and snow out of it with a breadknife. By now the sun had vanished behind the mountains and everything was in shadow.

The engine was completely dead.

I purposefully opened the bonnet, although a small voice inside me whispered that given my scant knowledge of engines, it was unwise to get my hopes up. Mat from Rosewood Bay would have known what to do. But the day my dad and I had replaced the radiator of my Renault 5 was ancient history, and my mechanical expertise had begun and ended there. All the same, I checked Eddie's radiator, which looked fine; if the only tool you have is a hammer, you tend to see every problem as a nail. By the light of the torch I had the impression that the battery had slipped a little, but the contacts looked corrosion-free. And there I stopped. I had exhausted my knowledge of engines. Even a tube of superglue couldn't help me this time.

Dusk had finally fallen and the snow was coming down thick and fast. A white carpet settled on the landscape, as if to soothe it.

No point worrying now, I told myself. Bloody cold though.

I went back inside to join Vera and the children. Within half an hour of breaking down, the temperature in the camper van had dropped so low that we could see our breath.

We had no choice but to spend the night there.

It was time for chocolate – our entire supply. We made tea to go with it and found a few food items that didn't need cooking. If the worst came to the worst, we could probably heat Eddie with the gas cooker (although admittedly, the gauge had been showing dark amber for two days). We had two LED torches and the dim emergency lighting was still working. Somewhere in Eddie's battery there must still have been a small spark of life.

For a while we sat and munched, the children busy with their chocolate, Vera and I sunk in thought, with no sound but the rustle of wrappers and noisy sips of hot tea. After our makeshift supper, we prepared for the night. We put on all our Salvation Army clothes and several pairs of socks each. I managed to get Mr Simon into two pairs of his own trousers and a pair of Nina's by picking him up by the waistband and jostling him up and down. By the end, he was giggling and barrel-shaped, so well-padded that his arms stuck out at his sides. His head was swathed in two hoods and a scarf, with only his eyes and the tip of his nose peeping out. His nose, I was glad to note, was a healthy red rather than black, and not too cold.

Another three-quarters of an hour later, the first drops of

condensation had frozen along the bottom of the back window, above the rubber seal.

'Great!' said Nina. 'Inside ice!' And she proceeded to make thumbprints all over the frosty glass. The outer side of the window was covered in snow.

It was as if we were in flight mode, no longer in touch with the outside world. We might have been on our way to another planet, with Eddie a kind of space probe that had lost contact with earth because it had travelled too far, or because the control station had failed to notice a comet (or maybe a ditch). Appropriately enough, he was parked at such an angle that we had to move around him at a slant, pulling ourselves along the cupboards, just like in a spaceship. All that was missing was the weightlessness.

There would be no more cars on the road that night. And despite the GPS that was presumably installed in hire vehicles like this, no one would know where we were; I suddenly remembered that the All Blacks were playing in the international Rugby Championship. The next morning, surely the first snowplough of the day would find us, with Eddie's nose sticking out into the road. I hoped the match had gone well; who knew, maybe even New Zealanders got cross sometimes. From what we'd seen of them so far this seemed unlikely, but perhaps under exceptional and devastating circumstances...

We took the mattresses from the bed above the driver's seat and piled them onto the mattresses in the back as insulation. A dank cold was rising from the floor and we were beginning to notice how draughty Eddie was. I couldn't get my hands properly warm.

Going to bed was, in any case, our only option.

'I don't want to go to bed.'

'Today's a bit special,' I say. 'Come on, in you get!'

'What about pyjamas?'

'No, today we're going to leave everything on and sleep like robbers.'

I told the obligatory bedtime story. This had to include a bear, a fox and a goose, only one of which was to be still standing at the end. This story was part of a long-running series and I'd used up all the vaguely plausible plotlines already. This instalment went on for quite a while – well over ten minutes, anyway: long enough to satisfy the children. I had really learned to take my time. Then there was nothing left to do.

Slowly, peace descended.

Because Eddie was at such an angle, we kept sliding on top of each other, a bundle of people and pillows, like animals huddled together at the far end of a dark den. Our four duvets lay heavy on us. I hoped no one was suffocating.

After a while, with the help of our combined body heat, Vera and I were no longer cold but we did feel pretty tired, maybe from the worry, which we hadn't altogether managed to hide from the children. Nina yawned and snuggled up against me. One of Simon's hands lay flung across my throat. It smelt of chocolate.

It was now pitch black in Eddie's belly. I don't think I've ever known such darkness. If I moved my hand in front of my face, I could feel a slight breath of air, but I couldn't see a thing. It was so dark that I wouldn't have noticed if all the things I couldn't touch in the van had ceased to exist. I reached out into the blackness. I could feel the smooth cold plastic cladding of Eddie's inside walls at my shoulder and the slightly damp curtain hanging just above my forehead. That there must be Vera's shoulder; at any rate, she gave a sleepy *hmm* when I touched it. And this was the icy back window with the frozen droplets squished flat by Nina. If I stretched my fingers right out, I could just about touch the table brackets on the wall next to the bed. But beyond that, nothing. Outside, too, all was quiet, apart from the occasional gust of wind. No light anywhere.

Our journey had come to a standstill in the middle of a wild, untamed landscape, I reflected. Before us, a jagged horizon rose thousands of metres into the snow-blown winter's night. There, beneath the sky, the mountains stood braced against time, buffeted by an angry wind that wounded itself over and over on the sharp crags. Further down, the crags gave way to plunging rock faces and scree slopes, out-of-reach places surrounded by grey, blurred contours. And water, frozen in mid-air.

Far below, on the more gently sloping hills where we were stranded, snow and darkness were forming their nightly alliance, pledging to wipe out all traces of mankind until morning, to return to an order far larger and older than humanity. But that night, at a nameless point in that expanse of nowhere, a tiny, fragile shell was lying, half-buried in snow, with four warm people inside. Maybe the snow and the night had overlooked us, or perhaps we were simply too small to bother them.

The wind died down. The snow had done its work. Silence settled on the countryside. The mountains had the world to themselves.

Close beside me, Nina jiggled herself into position again; it always took her ages to get comfortable. Eddie rocked a little and groaned.

Crazy, I thought. There's nobody here but us.

I listened in the darkness. For a moment there was complete silence.

But not for long. Out of the dark a voice whispered, 'Daddy?'

'Yes?'

'Are you there?'

'Yes.'

'So am I.'

'I thought you might be,' I whispered.

'And Mummy and Mr Simon are here, too.'

'Yes.'

'It's really nice and homey now, isn't it?' said Nina.

# LAKE TEKAPO

'HAVE YOU GOT A BUCKET?'

Nina stood in front of me, looking listless, even gloomy.

'What were you thinking of doing?' I asked.

'I need a bucket.'

I climbed into Eddie and fished out the green bucket from under the sink.

'Here you are. But don't forget we have to leave soon.'

'I know, it's all over,' she said truculently, taking the bucket without looking at me and stomping off. She could be quite a drama queen, especially when she thought she stood to gain by it. Maybe she was hoping for an extension to our trip.

We had been travelling for nearly two years and, even allowing for various arithmetic errors and problems of time difference, it was obvious that today or, at the very latest tomorrow, we would reach that millionth minute. We'd had a special breakfast that morning to celebrate, but Nina hadn't taken it well. In fact, our celebration had completely backfired. There had been freshly baked croissants with butter and strawberry jam, crispy muesli with honey and milk, and even freshly squeezed orange juice and hot chocolate. But Nina had only drunk half her mug of chocolate and then slunk off to the edge of the lake – a clear sign that she was upset. Mr Simon had taken care of the remains of the hot chocolate when no one was looking.

*   *   *

After our debacle in the mountains (we had been rescued without too many complications by a tow truck driven by an extremely cheerful mechanic, happy about the All Blacks' victory), we had decided not to be over-punctilious, but simply to celebrate when the moment seemed right.

A million minutes…

At the beginning of our travels I'd kept stopping to work out how much time we had left. I remembered how excited we'd been on Ko Phra Thong, 18,000 minutes into our trip – excited and a little scared that things might go wrong. At that point we'd been away for less than a fortnight; about the length of a longish holiday.

By the 60,000th minute, on Ko Yao Yai, we'd had nearly six weeks and had developed a more easy-going attitude to time. After 129,000 minutes (or three months) in Thailand, measuring time had become a kind of game. It was as if we were pinching ourselves to make sure we weren't actually dreaming.

What felt like an eternity later, in Port Douglas, we had been travelling for nearly six months – 242,000 minutes – and I only rarely stopped to count them. By the time we reached the Wallaby Creek Festival, after 630,000 minutes (over 14 months) of travel, I had, at last, come to trust my luck. I'd understood that time wasn't going to slip past when I wasn't looking. In the end, I stopped counting altogether. You can't always be ticking off the minutes of your life. Because at some point, our journey had become just that: time is simply another word for life.

A million minutes is a long time, but it all depends what you do with them. In my old life, a million minutes would probably have slipped between the lines of my to-do lists and been over before I had really registered that another two years had passed. On our journey, a million minutes was long enough to make a difference: by the end, nothing was the way it used to be. And we were well and happy. We had cause to celebrate.

Still, it had come as a shock to Nina when we'd told her that morning that the millionth minute had arrived. Vera and I lay in each other's arms, but when I turned to look at Nina, she was sitting hunched on the little camp chair, staring at the floor. Clearly, all she could think of was that the million minutes were over – gone, past, finished, never to return. I could understand her apprehension; after all, it had all been her idea and back then, when she'd conjured the words *a million minutes*, I imagined that she had purposely chosen a number so vast it appeared infinite, a number that seemed to go on and on without end; at least to a four-year-old with an extraterrestrial grasp of maths, who struggled even with numbers between one and 20. It wouldn't have occurred to her that such an unimaginably large number could be over in only two earth years. Not once in those two years had she asked us how long we'd been travelling or how much time we had left. That, too, is part of the paradise of childhood: each day is just another piece of infinity. More words of wisdom for my journal.

Of course, I too had mixed feelings, although mine were more concerned with the question of what would happen next. Vera and I still hadn't decided on a plan A, let alone a plan F or G. At the same time, though, it was clear that our journey wouldn't automatically end just because we'd be travelling less. Our experience had gone too deep for that. The more I thought about it, the more changes I came up with that would last beyond the end of the million minutes. I had a sneaky feeling that the Curitiba Man I had once been might not have recognised the new me.

Even more astonishing was the way our family of four had got to know one another. Is it absurd to talk about getting to know your own children? Both Simon and Nina were deeper and more complex than I'd imagined when we were going about our daily lives in Bonn. Every day I had watched them grappling with life, just like me – the same grappling and the same obstacles. They were, in turn, brave, despondent, curious, tricksy, wistful, angry, content. They were only half or a third my size, but they fought the same battles; like me, they enjoyed the lulls, chased after their goals. One day it flashed into my mind that we were all in the same boat, and although I knew that they had to find their own way through life, just being there with them every day had felt so right. Watching them grow had made me feel more connected to my family than I used to. As I had told Nina after I came last in the race: you never run alone.

The children, for their part, had got to know their parents much better, and I'd noticed how closely the pair of them watched us. They must have been able to see right through us by the end of our travels – not only as parents, but as people. Nina and Simon had seen me overexcited when we built rafts on Ko Phra Thong, lazy in the hammock on Ko Yao Yai and as thrilled as a child on my surfboard. They knew me as a problem-solver, a planner, a winner, a brick-maker, a bon vivant and a genuine loser; they had seen me on good days and bad, out of my depth, quarrelling, chopping wood, telling lies, haggling, exhausted, egoistic, stuck in a ditch, in love, uncertain, childish, sick, angry, wrong, doubtful, on a mission, contented...

We had changed in those million minutes, each of us individually and all of us together. We had become more of a family than I could ever have imagined.

I thought to myself: everything that is to come starts right here, right now. No end in sight.

*   *   *

I had done my best to explain all that to the children, although I soon realised that it wasn't a big deal for Mr Simon. His entire past had been *happy*. That was his word for anything he liked. There were *happy mornings*, *happy stories* and, most important of all, there was *happy Mummy*. With a life as happy as his, it was impossible to worry about the future. When I finally screwed up the courage to break it to him that we would soon be flying to a new country called Germany, his only reaction was to point purposefully at the freezer and say, 'Happy ice cream?'

With Nina it was more difficult. When I told her that our journey was, in a way, endless, she refused to accept it.

'You're just trying to comfort me,' she said, and proceeded to fire hard-nosed questions my way. Would we live in a house? That was relatively harmless, but it was only the beginning. Would I have to start earning lots of money again? We were now completely broke. I told her I'd like to do a bit of work, not because I wanted to earn lots of money again, but because it was interesting. Maybe at a school. Nina told me I was *quite often* good at playing with children; I should give it a go. But the interrogation wasn't over yet. Would we be able to spend the weekend in Port Douglas now and then? *Somebody* had to look after the emus and make sure their legs didn't get too thin. I said it was rather complicated.

'Oh,' Nina said. Then could she have a cat, at least? And when would we start travelling to other countries again? I said we had to settle in first. Her grandmas and grandads would be so pleased to see her and Simon! We'd be staying put for a little longer this time, that was all.

'You see! It's all over,' was her petulant summary of our exchange. There was no consoling her.

I tried another, simpler tack.

'That's life, I'm afraid,' I misfired.

Now Vera stopped pouring tea and threw me a look of disapproval. Nina glared at me in fury. Then she got up and stomped off to the edge of the lake.

It was no coincidence that we had chosen to spend the 'anniversary' of our time away on the shores of Lake Tekapo, which will always be a favourite place of mine. We had parked Eddie in such a way that we could eat breakfast looking out at the lake. If I think of New Zealand today, the first image that springs to mind is that surreal turquoise water, surrounded by the snow-covered mountains of the Southern Alps. I've never seen a colour like it.

What was most striking was the clarity. The air, the water, the colours, the light, the *fantatsic* weather, as Nina put it, and the contours of the snowy mountains against the steel-blue sky – everything around us was so clear. Even the darkness in Mackenzie Country is untroubled. There aren't many people in New Zealand and there isn't the idea that everything has to be illuminated, so the night sky comes all the way down to the ground; the universe seems to rest directly on the bare rocks. To get to the lake, we had coaxed Eddie over a pass to the campsite, which was on a small plateau. If you climbed onto one of the rocks up there, it felt as if the only thing connecting you to earth was the soles of your shoes; your body was already high in the dark universe. As you balanced there on the edge of the planet, only a last remnant of gravity prevented you from sailing off into space. I ought to speak to Nina about this, I thought. She might have a good idea. Maybe she'd suggest taking a running jump into the sky, all four of us at once, like astronauts taking those slow-motion steps on the moon…

It was there, on our first night at Tekapo, that I understood for the first time in my life what my father had been talking about when he'd tried to show me the Milky Way. As a child, I'd only ever seen a few scattered stars high up in the sky. True, some of them were in little clusters, but I couldn't see anything resembling a *way* and I couldn't see anything *milky*. I had drawn an imaginary zigzagging white line between the stars and decided that must be it. The epiphany came three decades later, here by Lake Tekapo. As I climbed the rock, I noticed that the stars weren't somewhere up above, but all around me, and there were even some shining *beneath* me on the horizon. It was dizzying. I stood still and waited for the dizziness to subside, and then, just as I thought it had gone, I saw the dazzling Milky Way, so vast that I caught my breath – a sparkling, blazing mass, stretching 100,000 light years from one horizon to the other; the whole mad universe in 3D. In colour, too – what seemed to be blue stars and green stars, red stars and purple stars, twinkling away like mad or slowly pulsating; shooting stars darting about all over the place, satellites languidly tracing their paths. In New Zealand it is quite impossible to conceive of the earth as being at the centre of anything. To the naked eye, it is clear that we are somewhere right on the very edge.

The handful of New Zealanders living on Lake Tekapo know how disorientated first-time tourists feel, and have thoughtfully put up signposts and information boards. Even the rocks are lovingly marked with little arrows to help you get your bearings when the landscape proves overwhelming. I once saw a large group of chattering Japanese tourists pile out of a bus and make their way towards the lake. The nearer they got, the slower and quieter they became until, at last, they stopped in complete silence at the edge of the shore. Their arms, holding their cameras, hung limp at their sides and for a few seconds of contemplation, almost no photos were taken. Anyone who has ever stood in front of the *Mona Lisa* or in the Sistine Chapel with a Japanese tour group knows that that is quite something.

Whoever built the little church here also understood that this is a place unlike any other. The church at Tekapo has neither an apse nor an altar, but a big window looking onto the water, so that the first thing you see when you enter is the lake. The only adornment is a simple wooden crucifix, so small that it doesn't detract from the view. Despite its plainness – or perhaps because of it – I thought it suited the church very well.

It was the colour of the water that impressed Nina more than anything. The day before our special breakfast, I went down to the shoreline to see what she was up to, and saw her holding a mineral water bottle up to the light. She was turning it this way and that and muttering, 'It must be somewhere in here! It can't have got out.'

Lake Tekapo looks as if someone has filled the enormous valley with thick turquoise paint, which is due to finely ground rock particles from the glaciers that feed it. It is so very turquoise that it's a real feat to imagine it colourless. I took a turn at filling Nina's bottle and the moment I pulled it out of the blue lake, full of non-blue water, I felt like a conjurer who opens his hand to reveal that the coin you were expecting has vanished. Nina and I had a playful discussion about how the blue was made and where it went to. We agreed that you had to be a little way away to see it and that it wasn't easy to catch. I kept my scientific knowledge of absorption spectra and wavelength to myself. It would have been a shame to spoil the moment.

*  *  *

Now I could see her in the distance, stumbling over the stones with her brimming bucket. With almost every lurching step, a little water slopped out over the rocks or onto her trousers.

'There! I'm taking this with me. As a sovereign of our journey,' she panted when she reached Eddie, her face set with wild resolve.

'As a what?'

'A thing you take with you,' she said, looking less confident.

'You mean a souvenir?'

'Yes.'

I glanced at the bucket. There was nothing in it but water.

She was fighting back tears.

'Come here,' I said.

'Now all the nice times are over!'

She was distraught. It wasn't the moment to ask her how she was thinking of transporting a bucket of water from New Zealand to Germany. She dodged me as I moved towards her, clearly in a real state.

I bit my lip. How could I explain to her that our million minutes wouldn't simply come to an end? That time like that is never lost? That memories stay inside us?

Nina's bucket reminded me of the Buddhist parable about how to rescue a drop of water from evaporation. Buddha suggested that his disciples put the drop into lakes, rivers or oceans. It was a little complicated, but worth a try.

'Fill your bucket with a million drops of water,' I told her.

'What?'

'Count carefully,' I said with a smile. 'Call me when you're ready!'

Shaking her head, she returned to the lake, spilling less than before because the bucket was almost empty. She was probably thinking what strange ideas I had. It occurred to me that if she took me at my word, we'd be here for a few more weeks and would need another 50 buckets.

I counted slowly backwards from a million. When I got to 999,982, I heard her call, 'Rea-dy!'

I joined her by the lakeside.

She was sitting next to the three-quarters-full bucket. If she'd put in any more, she wouldn't have been able to lift it.

'A million?' I asked. 'Did you count carefully?'

'Of course!' she said, with an impish look.

'Good. Now we're going to play a game, OK?'

'OK,' she said, without enthusiasm. She wasn't going to give in too easily, but I'd spotted a flash of curiosity in her eyes.

'All right then,' I said. 'In your bucket here are a million drops. Now for the game. Let's pretend that each of those drops was a minute, OK?'

That was how she and Mr Simon began. They spoke in the subjunctive of the game: *let's imagine we were…*

How easy it is to construct a parallel universe when you're a child. Grown-ups should try it, too: *Hello, let's imagine that our time is our life, OK?*

'Hmm,' was all she said, staring at the bucket as if to check what was inside.

'A bucket filled with a million minutes, OK?' I added. 'Each drop of water is a minute.'

'OK.' She nodded. She had no idea where I was headed, but I could tell she knew it was important to me.

'And the lake – how many minutes do you think are in there?'

We gazed at the huge expanse of bright blue lake, and at the purplish mountains beyond it. Such a beautiful wilderness. It was hard to imagine being back in the big city in Europe, I thought sadly.

'Lots and lots of millions?' she said.

Not bad, I thought. Today we will be working with numbers from one to lots and lots of millions.

'Yes,' I said. 'Probably even more. A billion. No, a trillion, or — shall we say a fantastillion?'

'Mhmm.' She nodded again, and it didn't look as if she were pretending.

'So, let's say that in this lake are all the minutes of your life, OK? Yesterday's minutes and today's and tomorrow's minutes and all the minutes when you're 20.'

'And when I'm 1,000,' said Nina, this time with a hint of enthusiasm. Not too much, though — I wasn't going to be allowed to forget that this was a really terrible day.

'That's right!' I said, feeling more buoyant myself. I seemed to be getting somewhere. 'Now, take the bucket and pour the million minutes into the lake, so that they will be with all the other minutes of your life!'

She looked at me in astonishment. 'Now?'

'Yes.'

'Can I fill it up again afterwards if it doesn't work?' she asked suspiciously.

'Of course you can,' I said.

She heaved up the bucket and tipped out the minutes.

We watched the silvery column hit the surface, making a dip in the water and producing little air bubbles that vanished after it. We watched it mingle with the lake until it was no longer visible. Of course, Nina also spilt a few minutes on her wellingtons and on the rocks, but I pretended not to notice.

'Like that?' she asked.

'Yes.'

Now for the nub of the matter. Even I was pretty excited. 'Are the million minutes gone?' I asked.

Nina stared at the calm surface of Lake Tekapo and screwed up her nose.

'They're in there,' she said, pointing at the water.

'And are they lost?'

'Hmm.'

'Give the lake a bit of a stir,' I said, handing her a piece of wood from the shore.

'What?'

'Give it a stir.'

She stirred clockwise and anticlockwise, half-heartedly at first, but more vigorously when she saw me nodding in encouragement.

'Where are the minutes now?' I asked.

Nina looked at me as if I was being foolish. 'They're still in there, all over the lake!'

'That's right! So our million minutes and the journey we've been on *are now inside your life*,' I said, spelling it out a bit. 'They haven't gone anywhere at all. Those million minutes haven't been lost. Now they're part of your life.'

For a while she watched the million minutes in the still waters.

Then she giggled. 'That's a funny trick,' she said, climbing onto my thigh.

'It's life,' I said.

Of course, I couldn't be sure how much had gone in, but she seemed pensive now, rather than upset. As we began to pack, she sat on a camp chair, sipping the second hot chocolate she'd asked for to make up for the morning's half-drunk cup, and staring dreamily at the epic lake. It was a start.

Time to set off.

Just this once, Nina was allowed to sit alongside us in the front passenger seat, because Mr Simon had already dropped off and would know nothing of the scandalous injustice of this concession, so we didn't need to worry that he would start asserting his rights or claiming compensation. And anyway, I wanted to do something to make Nina happy: she hadn't had an easy day.

The plan was to take Route 8 as far as Milton and then head from there to Dunedin, our final stop. After that, we would return to Christchurch. Our flight to Bonn was booked. From now on, our minutes really were numbered.

As we drove uphill on the bendy road, Lake Tekapo flashed beneath us one last time.

'Stop a moment, please,' I said.

Vera pulled Eddie over to the side of the road and cut the engine. We looked back at the magical view – the mountains, the water, the endless expanse of blue. None of us spoke.

It really is true that the slower you are, the more time you have. Speed melts away to give you more time. Moment by moment. Drop by drop. Maybe that's what Dalí was trying to tell us with those melting watches. Perhaps if all the watches in the world were to melt, we'd have a huge lake of time, calm and still, the beautiful blue water glistening in the sun, all the way to the horizon.

Eventually Vera broke the silence.

'That lake really is an incredible colour,' she said.

'That's because of all the happy minutes,' said Nina, still staring out of the window. 'The happiest minutes are blue.'

# LA VIDA ES UN CARNAVAL

## A B-ROAD NEAR COLOGNE (50°56'N, 6°52'E)
## RHINELAND, GERMANY

OUR FIRST WEEKS BACK IN GERMANY WERE FILLED with rain and hail and fog brought to us by an Atlantic low-pressure trough. As is often the way with Atlantic low-pressure troughs, it had sailed undisturbed over northern France and the plains of the Netherlands, thoughtfully holding back until it reached Germany. Such trough behaviour typically produces the leaden, overcast skies that ensure that Germans and the sun spend little time together between late September and early April. Thanks to a regrettable misalignment of the earth's axis, even the country's sunnier spots rarely manage to scrape together more than 1,700 hours of sunlight a year. Compare that with Perth in Australia, which easily clocks up 3,200 hours even in an off year, plus, of course, 43% light reflection from the sea. This means that the average Aussie living in Perth gets about twice as much light a year as the average German; 1,700 hours of sunlight is the equivalent of having the lights permanently dimmed.

This truth came rushing back to me when we pitched out camp in Bonn during the winter months. The gloom forces us Germans to spend half the year sitting in the semi-darkness of our houses, watching contemplatively as the raindrops trickle down the windowpanes, and such is the power of this enforced rumination that we have to be terribly careful not to slip into becoming writers or philosophers or composers. Heinrich Heine, Friedrich Nietzsche and Ludwig van Beethoven, to name but a few, were not mere accidents of cultural history, but owed their genius almost entirely to the early influence of the Bonn winter. It is perhaps the Germans' best-kept secret that their famous profundity is largely due to the foul weather.

Perhaps more surprising, though, than our climate-induced introspection, is the German capacity to make the most of life. Between the settlements of Cologne and Bonn, for instance, in the dreary despair of the perpetual Rhineland sleet, the atmosphere is second only to that at the Gaulish banquets of Asterix and Obelix. Cologne even has rules all of its own: the city's cheery optimism has been set in stone in the 'Cologne Constitution', a list of 11 edicts to guarantee total and perpetual cheerfulness. Six of the rules tell you that things are the way they are and you're best accepting that, and the other five tell you how to have fun with your fellow human beings (with specific reference to drinking, having sex and laughing). Cologne should be the favourite city of every happiness researcher in the universe.

Of course, there's also a whole string of laws in Germany, some of which took some getting used to after such a long time abroad. One of these was a ridiculous traffic regulation demanding that all drivers in Germany drive on the other – which is to say the right – side of the road.

In theory, I was aware of this when, early one Sunday morning, I was driving along a lonely B-road south of Cologne; suddenly, a car emerged from a neglected beet field, apparently hell-bent on collision.

For a second I told myself that the driver of the silver metallic Passat Comfortline must still be asleep. But instead of getting off the side of the road I firmly believed to be my own, he began to sound his horn more and more insistently. Another second later, we both slammed on our brakes and skidded towards each other in surreal slow motion. By this time my foot was on the floor, but instead of the horrific crash I was expecting, I heard a dull crunch from the direction of my bumper.

Now both cars were stationary on the left side of the road, sideways on to one another. The driver of the other car opened his door and the voice of Marlene Dietrich filled the cool morning air. An elderly indigenous male got out. There could be no doubt about his origins as a native of the Rhineland. The sea-lion moustache, for one thing, but also the fact that he'd been driving in a hat and coat. Unless he'd spent the night in the car, that crumpled beige coat was an unequivocal indicator of his ethnic identity.

'What planet are you from?' he said, staring first at his car and then at me.

I couldn't open my door, which must have been knocked out of shape in the collision. The man went round the back of his car – there was no room at the front – and knocked on my window.

What a mess. I'd been back in Germany a mere matter of weeks and although this was my first literal car crash, I couldn't claim it was my first accident of the day. Only that morning I'd knocked a pot of cream from the top shelf of a very full fridge. Since I'd stopped converting my time into world travel, I seemed to be on the look-out for new time-filling strategies. I had turned up an incredible four hours late to Mr Simon's kindergarten interview – there were 68 applications for only 14 places – and days before that, I had left Nina's gym bag on the underground and blamed her.

'Look here, young fellow, are you still asleep or something?' The man was now in front of my window.

'I've got F43,' I mumbled. Then, loud enough for him to hear, I said, 'I can't open the door.'

And my seatbelt was jammed – probably something to do with the way I'd slammed on the brakes. Knowing this was self-inflicted, I slumped in my seat.

*  *  *

It was Anna Amsel who had suggested with her usual directness that I might be suffering from F43. I didn't go to see her for almost three weeks after getting back to Bonn. There's always a danger with psychologist friends that you will alienate them by spewing all your undigested problems onto them.

'How lovely that you're back!' she had said.

I had asked her for a towel because my bike saddle was soaked with 'wet stuff from the sky'. Then we'd exchanged news, but it must have been obvious what kind of mood I was in.

'So, tell me how you are,' she said eventually.

'Not great.' It came bursting out of me. 'I keep screwing up. I have to do all this strange stuff I don't really want to do – there are all these practical to-do lists. And I can't sleep because I lie in bed brooding about everything we've done and what the hell we're doing now.'

'F43! A particularly dramatic variant,' said Anna Amsel with a grin.

'I'm sorry?'

'ICD F43. So-called adjustment disorder following an extremely stressful experience.'

'Aha,' I said. ICD stands for the International Statistical Classification of Diseases and Related Health Problems, a medical classification list compiled by the World Health Organization. I mulled over the incredible remote paradises we had visited in Thailand, Australia and New Zealand. Neither Vera nor I had worked for two years, and we had just come back from a dream trip of a lifetime. 'And what extremely stressful experience might that be?'

'Ever heard of *re-entry shock*?' Anna asked, angling a thick red book out of her bookcase. 'It's… hang on, I'll read it to you. The lesser-known fifth phase of culture shock… No, that's not the bit I'm looking for. Blah blah blah… Here it is. According to Woesler, re-entry shock – which is when we return to our own culture – is generally more challenging than the original culture shock. It's an experience that we're psychologically unprepared for. Sound familiar?'

'I'm still settling in,' I said. 'Last week I met up with a friend, Bernd – you know Bernd, don't you? He was completely overworked, pasty-faced and he'd put on weight, and when I asked him how he was, he wouldn't tell me. He just said, "Oh, you know, certain things have to be done in life." And he laughed this funny laugh, as if he'd said something funny. And then he didn't say anything else. As if he'd answered my question.' I shook my head. 'I've been asking myself ever since if he was right. Do certain things have to be done in life?'

'How are the kids?' was Anna Amsel's only response. Was she dodging my question? She probably couldn't come up with a smart answer.

'I think it's just another stop on the line for Nina and Simon – all new and exciting. They take everything so lightly. The only trouble is getting them out of bed in the morning. Trying to wake Nina *in the midnight*, as she says, is purgatory. Like you, she thinks I have an adjustment disorder, only she'd say I've over-adjusted.' I laughed. 'But basically, the pair of them have settled in nicely. It's a kind of game for them. No F43 in sight.'

'Exactly – because it's a kind of game! But you've chosen to play the game as well: you have good reasons for being here in Bonn for the time being.'

'So you agree with Bernd, that certain things have to be done?' I asked.

Anna Amsel put down the book. 'It may not seem like it right now, but you're free to choose what game you play. You may not be able to change the rules, but you can choose the game. And you're lucky because you learned so many different new games while you were away. Being spoilt for choice is a gift.'

I looked at Anna doubtfully. 'You're not serious, are you?'

'Yes, I am! Now you can finally make a conscious decision to do something, or not to do it. No more excuses. You can buy yourself a ticket and take up one of those dream jobs you were always telling me about in your emails. What were they again? Manager-bootcamp-leader? Driftwood-seller? Namer of beaches, broken chocolate-dealer, flight assistant? Or you can put that off for the moment and stay here for a bit. Or apply for a job at the UN. Nothing *has* to be done. Not the way I think you mean it.'

I nodded cautiously. Of course, her answer was pretty much what I wanted to hear. The trouble was that ever since getting back, I'd been suffering from an acute lack of ideas. I wasn't going to be starting a new game any time soon.

But Anna Amsel hadn't finished. I should have known there was more coming, as she never gives simple answers. She probably suffers from severe *déformation professionnelle*: the tendency to view life from the point of view of one's profession.

'One more thing,' she said. 'I do think that once you've decided what you want to play, you ought to stick to the rules. That does have to be done.'

I muttered something about psychologists and other soul-sellers. 'Really, you're all the same. You sound just like Dr Finkelbach.'

'How about considering a teeny scrap of practical advice for a change?' Anna asked, smiling at me.

'And what might that be?' I asked sniffily.

'You don't have to believe that the wet stuff that falls from the sky is just rain, but it might be a good idea to equip yourself with a saddle cover for your bike. You bought factor 50 suncream when you were in Australia, didn't you?'

I laughed. I was already feeling a little better, but I didn't let it show too much; Anna Amsel wasn't going to be allowed to forget that, for me, this was a really terrible day.

'I suppose I could also install a ball pool for flying dogs in our back garden, next to the bikes.'

'You could indeed. But that would be another kind of game altogether.'

It was a typical Anna Amsel exchange. After a conversation like this, I'd sometimes ring her a few weeks later and say: *now* I understand what you were getting at.

\* \* \*

Meanwhile the knocking on my car window had grown more insistent.

'Hello? Aren't you well? Is something the matter? I can't hear you!' The man was holding his hand cupped behind his ear. He was the kind of person the indigenous people here call *a character*. And a character is quite a godsend when you've caused a minor accident – a good deal less dangerous, for instance, than an ambitious, Barbour-clad banker in his mid-30s.

'Hello!'

'I can't open the door!' I yelled, rattling the door handle.

'Maybe you should try pulling up the little knob,' the man called, waving his finger at it. He had a point. It's generally a good idea to unlock a door if you're thinking of trying to open it. It opened with no trouble at all and I got out. My legs were trembling.

'I'm terribly sorry,' I stammered.

The man looked at me, sizing me up. 'What on earth were you doing driving on the wrong side of the road?'

'That's quite a long story,' I said, clearing my throat. 'A million minutes long, to be precise.'

'All right. You don't need to tell me now. The main thing is that we're both in one piece. And we can still laugh!'

He straightened his hat and inspected his car. Its silver bumper was striped dark green from Vera's old Corsa. The mark looked a little like a gecko. We both stooped to inspect the damage. The man reached out a fingernail and scratched.

'Hmm,' he said, staring at the green paint on his nail.

I nodded mentally, supposing that the *hmm* was his way of preparing me for what was coming next. Repainting a bumper could cost a fortune – at least, when it needed repairing as well. I had a sneaky suspicion that it was the kind of bumper that beeped hysterically when you drove too close to it.

A friend had recently been in a similar position. He hadn't, of course, been driving on the wrong side of the road, but the police report described him as the *clear originator of an approximately six-centimetre-long discoloration on the bumper of vehicle owner F.* As the originator told me in disbelief, apparently you can't simply paint over a mark like that, because the colours might clash: the new paint might be a different shade from the rest of the front bodywork. But repainting the whole of the front of the car isn't a solution either, because then it might not match the sides. All you can do is switch off your brain and completely replace the front bodywork. My friend ended up paying the equivalent of 20,000 minutes, which luckily included the labour cost.

'That'll be €3,000,' the man said gravely.

I looked at him in indignation and he burst out laughing. He was a cheerful soul. Nevertheless, I felt my left eyelid twitch uncontrollably.

'My wife'll sort it out,' he said. 'She has a knack for fixing that kind of thing.'

'I'll give you my phone numbers,' I said, fishing a pen and some paper out of the glove compartment and scribbling them down.

The man looked at the paper. 'Ah, so you live in Bonn?'

'At the moment. Well, kind of – for the time being,' I said, tying myself in knots.

'Yes, I could tell you were new here. There's something different about you. Maybe you're a little too serious… It'll soon pass, I'm sure.'

He dug in his coat pocket and pressed a menthol sweet wrapped in green paper into my hand. 'People here always say, "Don't take things too seriously!" You should remember that.' He eyed me sharply again, as if wondering whether I was likely to take his advice. 'But you do know how to start a car, don't you?'

I must have looked at him desperately, because he began to roar with laughter. 'Don't forget to laugh, young fellow – very important. Rule number one, I always say: *don't forget to laugh*. Life's a carnival.'

I agreed, nodding and smiling. A resident of Cologne ought to know. In Rio de Janeiro a carnival is to be expected, but to pull off a carnival in Cologne or Bonn during a harsh Rhineland winter is something of a miracle. Also known as the *fifth season*, the Rhineland carnival acts as a bright overlay to the gloomier months of the year and traditionally starts at 11 minutes past 11 on the 11th day of the 11th month. Other German tribes have developed similar customs to help themselves through the trickier seasons – the Munich Oktoberfest is a world-famous example.

The man grinned at me and pointed at the road ahead of us. 'It's pretty straightforward. First, you have to decide which way you want to go. Then you have to keep an eye out for the signposts. If you ever find yourself looking at the back of a signpost, you're on the wrong side of the road. No matter what planet you're from.'

At that moment, something shifted inside me and my gloomy mood lifted. We must have offered a strange sight to the crows as they flew back and forth over the misty fields: a pair of men standing at the roadside next to their cars, chuckling away together under a grey sky. My rubbery legs had steadied themselves again.

*   *   *

When I got home, I went straight to Vera. It was her car, after all. The children were playing outside, oblivious to my guilt. 'I had a little accident. Your left bumper is now ever so slightly rounded off at the front and has a silver finish,' I said.

She stared at me. 'But you're all right?'

'Well, er, yes.'

'Everything in working order?'

I nodded. 'Although the gauge might need readjusting.'

'The car's or yours?'

'Very funny.'

'Listen, I have to finish what I'm working on,' she said. 'Can you check on the kids? You don't know where the cream is, do you?'

I mumbled something about having a very hard time and Vera gave me one of those kisses that make everything all right again. Then I went out into the garden.

Nina and Mr Simon were playing very intently in the sandpit. It looked like a good mixture of earthy and homey – there was even a bowl of sandy strawberries perched on the edge of the pit.

'Will you play with us?' Nina called immediately.

'Yes!' Mr Simon cried.

I hesitated. 'What are you playing?'

Nina shot me a look of disbelief. 'Can't you see?' She pointed at the sandpit and waited for me to tell her what was going on.

'Island?' I asked.

She nodded, satisfied. Then she jerked her head towards Mr Simon.

'He's the captain,' I said.

Again, she nodded, as if congratulating herself on having brought me up so well.

Oh dear, I thought. For days they'd been playing a game in which a fortunate captain discovered an island inhabited by a strawberry-owning princess. My role was either to kidnap the princess or to steal her strawberries, but I didn't feel like playing the bad-tempered sailor who ran away with one or the other. I wouldn't manage to be *real* enough today; I wouldn't even reach Level 2.

'Um, maybe we could play a different game?' I asked tentatively, not wanting to spoil their fun. I just had to come up with a new story idea. Surely I could manage that after so much practice?

'Course we can!' said Nina, in soothing tones. 'And do you know what?'

'No,' I said.

'You'll never guess!' she said, giggling.

'No, I don't suppose I will,' I said with a grin.

She was beaming from ear to ear.

'Now I have a million ideas!'

# EPILOGUE

## WHAT'S WET AND FALLS FROM THE SKY?

'WELCOME,' THE DOG SAID AFFABLY. 'JUST A FEW SHORT questions, then we're done.'

'Oh, dear me,' Dr Finkelbach groaned. He looked down at himself. He was still in one piece and sitting in a rather large office chair, clutching his briefcase. The dog sat behind an imposing desk with a pen in its paw.

Only a moment before, he'd been standing at his car door about to head for home. He'd had a tiring day at work and that little girl had just about finished him off. 'Unbelievable,' he'd muttered to himself as he dug around in his briefcase for the car keys. 'What's wet and falls from the sky? A dog!' Then he'd heard a strange noise overhead and looked up to find a wet dog hurtling towards him.

The next thing he knew, he was in an office with this dog, feeling distinctly dizzy.

'Where am I?'

'Don't worry,' the dog said soothingly. 'You'll soon have the chance to talk everything over with the person in charge. These are mere formalities.' It smiled. 'All right then: where do you come from?'

'Bonn! I'm from Bonn. Listen, I…'

'Just a moment, please. I must make a note of that. Planet: Bonn. Is that right? With two ns?'

'Bonn's a city, not a planet! What is all this?'

'Ah, that was my next question. How many days were you thinking of staying here? Do you have a connecting ticket?'

'Listen, I urgently need to talk to someone.'

'By all means. That's what we're here for. *No stresstic.* If you could just wait while I complete this admissions form. You know how it is.' The dog winked conspiratorially at Dr Finkelbach. 'Bureaucracy.'

'You must have the wrong person. I'd like to go back to my car.'

'First some questions. So, what's wet and falls from the sky?' the dog asked.

'Excuse me?'

'It's very wet' – the dog paused meaningfully – 'and it falls from the sky.' The animal spoke with emphatic slowness, sketching a large circle in the air with its paws and glancing first at the ceiling and then back at Dr Finkelbach. 'We have to run you through this test,' it added. 'It's for your own good.'

'Rain, of course. And now maybe you could tell me…'

The dog smiled indulgently. 'Rain? That's a good one. Very amusing. Try again!'

'Excuse me?'

'Now look here. This won't do at all, you know.' Another wink. 'Listen: it's *wet* and it falls from the *sky.*'

'We call it rain,' Dr Finkelbach said, looking at the dog with a mixture of despair and indignation and running his left hand *innervously* over his briefcase.

'I see… So it wasn't a joke? Tell me, do you understand gravity?'

'What do you think? I'm from Earth. Who are you anyway? You look like a…' Dr Finkelbach gazed at the creature, who was busy making notes in a journal. 'You bear a certain resemblance to a dog, except you can speak! How is that even possible?'

'Very well observed,' the dog said mockingly. '*Canis nina-ensis.*' He fluttered a paw. 'Pleased to meet you. And you?'

'*Homo sapiens,*' Dr Finkelbach stuttered. 'I'm a psychologist.'

'Ah,' said the dog with a chuckle. 'That would explain the gravity.'

It scratched its head. 'Old Earth. Far corner of the Milky Way. Met someone from there once before. Robert Steiner or something.'

'Rudolf. Rudolf Steiner,' Dr Finkelbach croaked.

'That's the one! Do you know him?'

'Not personally,' Dr Finkelbach groaned. 'What the hell is…'

'He was trying to get from India to Atlantis, but got in a bit of a muddle and ended up in Western Australia,' the dog went on. 'Then he succumbed to the Antipodean sun… Insisted all his life that he'd discovered the southern route to Scandinavia. He founded a little settlement down there – Rosewood Bay, or something.'

'This isn't Bonn, is it?' Dr Finkelbach panted, little beads of sweat gathering on his brow. He was still clutching the briefcase and wriggled around on the seat, trying to get comfortable.

The door opened and a man in white robes came in. He was wearing a bandana around his head and looked like Charlton Heston as Moses in *The Ten Commandments*. He wandered around the room, whistling, then suddenly spotted Dr Finkelbach.

'Oh, sorry. I didn't know you were busy,' he said to the dog. The dog leant back in its chair and turned away from Dr Finkelbach, so he couldn't see its muzzle. Looking at the man in white, the dog rolled its eyes towards his interviewee and mouthed the word *Earth*.

The man in white nodded. He went up to Finkelbach, gave him the once-over and held out his hand.

'Morx is the name. Karl Morx. What can we do for you?'

'I want to go back to my car!'

Morx and the dog exchanged glances.

'He doesn't seem to know the password,' the dog said gravely.

'Of course he doesn't,' Morx replied. 'He wouldn't still be here if he did.'

'Look here,' Dr Finkelbach said, deliberately jovial, 'I don't want to cause you any…'

'What's wet and falls from the sky?' Morx asked, friendly but firm.

Dr Finkelbach folded his arms across his chest and stuck out his lower lip.

'Dog,' he said tersely.

The dog breathed a sigh of relief. 'Not very original, is it?' it said apologetically, tapping itself on the chest.

'Never mind,' said Morx. 'We're getting there.'

'I want to speak to a lawyer immediately,' Dr Finkelbach shouted.

'We're the Parallel Universe Dream Agency. Congratulations! You can wish for whatever you want!'

'I don't understand...' Finkelbach stammered.

'You're free to dream here.'

'I don't want to dream. I want my car keys. I must have left them in the door.'

'You don't want to dream?' Morx asked incredulously.

'Certainly not,' Dr Finkelbach said. 'I'm a therapist!'

'All right then.' The dog shrugged, and gazed across at Morx.

'Hang on!' said Dr Finkelbach. 'Can I really have *anything* I want in this parallel universe?'

'Of course!' Morx said, and the dog nodded confirmation.

'I always wanted to go to Lake Tekapo in New Zealand someday,' Dr Finkelbach said softly.

'Oh, I'm sorry,' Morx said despondently. 'I'm afraid we've taken the phrases *always wanted* and *someday* out of the programme. We've done the sums, and it simply doesn't work out. The realisation period can be up to a billion days, you know?'

Dr Finkelbach stared long and hard at the dog. For the first time he leant back a little in his chair. Then he said, hesitantly, 'Now would be good, too.'

'Great. That's more realistic. Would you write that at the top of your to-do list, please?' The dog passed over a pen and piece of paper.

'Yes, of course,' said Dr Finkelbach. He wrote on the paper and handed it back.

At that moment, he heard a strange noise overhead. The next thing he saw was his own face smiling delightedly in the rear-view mirror of his car. A piece of paper was stuck to the mirror with sticky tape. Right at the top in point-32 font it said: *To do: Tekapo*. That was all.

'Recalculating route,' the satnav voice suddenly whined. Then it coughed. 'Excuse me. This may take some time. It's not exactly round the corner… OK, now I've located it.'

Dr Finkelbach was still staring in the mirror, his hands on the wheel.

'Ready?' the satnav asked.

Dr Finkelbach nodded. *Swowly*. 'I'm ready,' he said.

# AFTERWORD

I DON'T THINK IT WOULD TAKE ANYONE MORE THAN a couple of seconds to come up with some essential ingredients for happiness: a sufficient supply of food, the absence of pain, people who care about you, enough sleep, etc. But although time is as essential as any of the above, I feel we tend to overlook its importance. Time is the substance that life is made of. Living without time would be like painting on air.

Even though our lifetime is so precious, we spend it as if it were toy money, of which we have suitcasesful. But what if we – hypothetically speaking – considered our life to be the only one we have, and then – of course, also only hypothetically speaking – accepted that this life was terminal? Would you live your life as you have done over the last 12 months? And what do *you* want to be when you grow up?

I am so grateful that Nina asked me these questions.

After *One Million Minutes* had reached the bestseller lists in Germany, an interesting debate emerged on social media. Someone suggested that I must be one of those snotty stuck-up rich prigs who simply don't know what to do with all their money. I was surprised, as we were chronically broke after our trip, and are still paying off our loan. We will probably never own our own property.

It is not easy to have no financial security (gazillions of people in Germany alone know what I am talking about). I say this without any bitterness and only to highlight my belief that dreams don't come for free. My dear friend Anna Amsel hit the nail on the head: choose your path and pay the price. It's quite existential: as long as you are willing to accept that there will be a price, you have the freedom to make the decisions you want.

I am eternally grateful that we decided to use our loan to buy the best time of our lives, instead of a car and home improvements. The furniture we were going to buy would by now be virtually worthless, whereas our million minutes now classify as an amazing life experience that has given us priceless memories!

I guess that regarding the issue of time, most of us ordinary mortals, especially those who will not inherit, have to make a deliberate choice between generating wealth and creating an abundance of time. Do I want the new car plus carport, or would I rather like to have Thursday afternoons off to go to the mountains or the sea with my wife? Do I absolutely need the wafer-thin flat screen TV and the latest smartphone, or do I head to the playground with my son straight after school on Mondays? Will I still need to make money 42 hours a week when I'm 60, or will I finally do some of the things that I've always wanted to do? Oh and by the way, this is also very important to me: I think there is a big difference between having to make money and wanting to work. I guess it is very important to do the job you love, as you may spend about a third of your life doing it.

What else has happened since our million-minute trip?

It may not surprise you that there was no happy-ever-after. I, for example, did compromise on what I had learned during our journey from time to time. But at least there was a different-ever-after. None of us believed in the concept of normality again, although we haven't (yet) become outlaws. For six months, I eagerly experimented with home schooling, which everyone else in our family thought was pretty stupid. Nina said she would rather attend an ordinary school than do a single sun salutation on the beach with me. I have learned how to juggle (albeit only with four balls), and I now know some impressive extraterrestrial maths.

Obviously, my career went down the drain when I chose the million-minute trip. I can probably count myself lucky there as well, or I'd still be sitting in gigantic arenas amid the senseless loop of sepulchral conferences. Old colleagues have assured me that everything is just the same as it always was in Curitiba.

Michael has moved to a place where the wind is stronger. Beany is now a photographer. Nina's doctor gives impressive talks that feature flying dogs. Phoenix calls himself The Enlightened. Ko Phra Thong has had one holiday resort built after another; industrial tourism is infiltrating the most remote corners of the world and prices have exploded – much of our trip would be unaffordable now. Steffi and John got married in Rosewood Bay. Sabrina and her daughter Lou are sailing around the world. Jim is now specialising in Bulgarian women.

Recently a good friend of ours died of cancer: the last thing he wrote to us was that we should enjoy our lives.

Lake Tekapo is just as still as it always was. The other day a film company promised to get this thing about the million minutes onto the big screen. I already know what Nina will say when she sees her first flying dog.

I am sorry to say that you will never find Rosewood Bay, because I made a promise to the friends we made who want to keep their wonderful home a secret.

The only thing that I regret about our long journey is that I lost out on the opportunity to work in South Africa – which is why I work at a school in South Africa now (although fairies are not part of my daily life). That is another adventure.

By now the children have their own networks of friends, so long trips are out of the question for us, even if we could afford them. Simon can't wait until he's able to run faster than I can – and it won't take much longer. I have forgotten how to win; by now, it seems more inconvenient than losing.

Simon and some keen readers have noted that he doesn't have much to say in this book. This is solely due to his age-specific language scope at the time of our travels. By now, I have learned so much from you, Simon: thank you! I think that we adults are in urgent need of supervision by qualified children – nine-year-olds like Simon who aren't deluded by disillusionment. We need those small people who wear their hearts on their sleeves and catch us out with all the right questions, who think everything is possible: flying dogs, endless love, immortality and freedom. All we have to do is listen properly!

In Nina's case, it was easy. When your child is equipped with so many letters from medical personnel, it is difficult to turn a blind eye (or rather a deaf ear) to them. It is also morally impossible to be impatient with someone who has a disability, let alone a girl who is *swowness* personified. From time to time 'I was struggling with myself,' as Nina would put it, and she was right: actually, the irritating thing is that you only get irritated with yourself. Nina, meanwhile, is doing very well. It doesn't look like she will ever experience real stress, be able to tell the time properly, eat on the go or strive to be boringly realistic. If I sometimes slip back into Curitiba Man or any other prestigious being, she is quick to quote me excerpts from this book to ensure that I leave the path of reason as quickly as possible. After all, I wrote it myself, right?

So, stay well – and take your time! No stresstic!

And now, Nina and Simon: what are we going to do next?

# ACKNOWLEDGEMENTS

It takes a lot of time and a whole village to bring up a father; my sincere thanks to everyone I met along the way. I have been very lucky.

*   *   *

I should also like to thank our hosts and friends who made the first million minutes of our journey so unforgettable – especially Jason and Maren, Nina and the Wild Three, Sofia and Ema, Sarah and Will, Yamalia and Katja, George and Janelle.

Thank you, Maria, Klaus and Bernolf for inspiring talks. Thank you, Michael and Beany – I wish you 6 Beaufort. Thanks to Glenn and Mark for the relaxing times in Origin.

Special thanks go to Dominic for some of the doodles, especially the lovely something-grinder, and to Meike for helping me with understanding my own English.

Special thanks also go to the Penguin team and to Hanna and Ulla, who made this book possible. Thanks also to Natalie for commissioning and supporting the book's English edition, to Sadie for patiently editing and revising it for English publication, to Kate for her help throughout the editorial process, and to Imogen for the translation.